OLIVER ST JOHN GOGARTY
The Real Buck Mulligan

OLIVER ST JOHN GOGARTY
The Real Buck Mulligan

GUY ST JOHN WILLIAMS

SOMERVILLE PRESS

Somerville Press Ltd,
Dromore,
Bantry,
Co. Cork,
Ireland P75 NY22

First published 2022

The author wishes to thank Veronica Jane O'Mara for her kind permission to quote from the writings of Oliver St John Gogarty.

Designed by Jane Stark
Typeset in Adobe Garamond Pro
seamistgraphics@gmail.com

ISBN: 978-1-8382544-4-5

Printed and bound in Spain
by GraphyCems, Villa Tuerta, Navarra

To Milady

FOREWORD

The Real Buck Mulligan

W.B. Yeats proclaimed him "one of the great lyric poets of our age" and endorsed this claim by including 17 of Oliver St John Gogarty's poems in *The Oxford Book of Modern Verse* which he edited in 1936. They remained friends and it is said that Gogarty was responsible for ensuring Yeats a seat in the first Irish Senate.

Conversely James Joyce portrayed Gogarty as "Stately, plump Buck Mulligan" in the opening lines of his masterpiece *Ulysses*. Superficially the description can be seen as complimentary, but it is not. The "stately" is a poke at Gogarty's establishment status and the "plump" is a jeer at his perceived self-regard.

So, which of these literary giants is correct? Can Joyce's bitter portrayal of Gogarty as the minor character Malachy "Buck'" Mulligan in *Ulysses* be accurate or is Yeats's marked admiration of his friend and his poetry a clearer endorsement of the man? *The Real Buck Mulligan* by Gogarty's grandson Guy St John Williams tackles these questions in a more accurate portrayal of this somewhat enigmatic Irish figure of the first half of the twentieth century.

What is known about Oliver St John Gogarty is that he was a celebrated, Dublin professional man who packed several lives into one. He was a classical lyric poet, an accomplished sportsman, an ear, nose and throat surgeon, a Republican, a Senator and an author. He was also a renowned wit, although this latter trait could display a vicious element which cost him several friendships.

He said that he preferred to "have people better than myself about me". He was born into an upper-class medical family which ensured his inclusion in Dublin society, but he cultivated his standing among the Irish literary establishment through his lyric poetry which was held in high regard. He was not just a close associate of W.B. Yeats but also George Moore, AE (George Russell) and James Stephens amongst others.

During his time as a medical student Gogarty had witnessed the appalling living conditions of Dublin's under classes when tending patients in the tenement buildings. This inspired him to write a three-act play *Blight* which he set in a tenement dwelling, with characters drawn from his own experience and in so doing called attention to the state's perennial housing failings. *Blight* played for a week in the Abbey Theatre to packed houses. One of the performances was attended by Sean O'Casey and it was from *Blight* that O'Casey drew inspiration for his renowned Dublin trilogy *Shadow of a Gunman*, *Juno and the Paycock* and *The Plough and the Stars*. Before putting pen to paper O'Casey sought Gogarty's approval to develop the theme and permission was duly granted.

Despite fraternising with the Anglo-Irish establishment, Gogarty was a lifelong Republican and a member of the Irish Republican Brotherhood. He was a close associate of both Arthur Griffith and Michael Collins and embalmed both men on their deaths. (In analysing Collins's corpse, Gogarty concluded that he had been killed, not by a direct hit, but by a ricochet bullet thereby offering one answer to the eternal question of who killed Michael Collins.)

In an attempted reprisal for his political associations, in January 1923, Gogarty was abducted from his Dublin home in Ely Place by anti-Treaty forces and taken to a house near Chapelizod in Co. Dublin. In a dramatic escape he plunged into the freezing floods of the river Liffey and was swept downstream. W. B. Yeats wrote of the abduction:

". . . Oliver Gogarty was captured by his enemies, imprisoned in a deserted house on the edge of the Liffey with every prospect of death. Pleading a natural necessity he got into the garden, plunged under a shower of revolver bullets as he swam the ice-cold stream and promised it, should it land him in safety, two swans. I was present when he fulfilled that vow."

Alongside his political activities, the success of Gogarty's medical practice in Dublin had earned him his first fortune with which he bought a second home, Renvyle House in Connemara. He had married Martha (Neenie) Duane of Moyard, Co. Galway and during that courtship he had developed an enduring love of Connemara. However, in February 1923, anti-Treaty forces continued to wreak revenge on former political opponents and due to Gogarty's affiliations with the pro-Treaty side, de Valera's henchmen burned Renvyle House to the ground.

In the autumn of 1939 after, but not due to, a libel case associated with his first prose work *As I Was Going Down Sackville Street*, Gogarty left Ireland for the United States and did not return until 1946 thereafter visiting his home country on a bi-annual basis. He collapsed from a heart attack on a New York street in 1957 and died in the Beth Israel Hospital three days later.

The extent to which Gogarty is remembered today can be attributed to two biographies of him. The first *A Poet and His Time*s was written by Ulick O'Connor and published by Jonathan Cape in 1964. The second biography was written by Professor J. (Jack) B. Lyons of the Royal College of Surgeons, entitled *Oliver St John Gogarty: The Man of Many Talents* published by Blackwater Press in 1980.

In this third biography we meet *The Real Buck Mulligan* written by his grandson Guy St John Williams. As a child Guy knew his grandfather, but he gleaned more information from his mother Brenda, who was Gogarty's daughter and also from his uncle Oliver (Noll) one of Gogarty's two sons.

The Real Buck Mulligan is a fascinating and comprehensive portrait of one of the leading characters of Ireland's newfound Irish Republic. On these pages, Guy Williams has provided the reader with an informative, insightful, enjoyable and above all reliable account of one of the nation's perhaps neglected, but important literary and political figures of the early twentieth century.

Roger Greene
September 2022

INTRODUCTION

"Had Oliver St John Gogarty not existed, James Joyce would have invented someone else to play the role of friend and betrayer in life and in fiction. But had Oliver Gogarty not existed, had a different rival been found at the appropriate moment, *Ulysses* would not be precisely the book that it is. Joyce's comic masterpiece, in mood and motif, bears some significant traces of the man who served as the model for Buck Mulligan. Gogarty's relation to Joyce and his work – he was once described as 'accessory before the fact' of *Ulysses* – deserves another look."[1]

A decade elapsed before Dr J. B. Lyons provided his answer with his thoughtful and wryly observant biography *Oliver St John Gogarty – The Man of Many Talents*. Jack Lyons appreciated that his subject had been traduced. "His characterization as 'Buck Mulligan' in James Joyce's *Ulysses* served him ill, that brilliant but malicious portrait masking a kinder and more sensitive personality."

However, just as he had in life, so also in death, Oliver St John Gogarty eluded interpretation, defied understanding, much as James Carens had predicted that he might. "And then there is the oddest paradox of all: it is that for a man who lived so public a life, played so many roles, and contributed so enthusiastically to the legend he became, Gogarty very firmly drew lines in what he wrote beyond which he would not permit the public or his readers to pass . . . and much of his most personal and private experience never entered into his autobiographical books." Carens quoted Gogarty's own evasive words: "Beyond Reynolds' Introduction to my book of verse, there are hardly any facts of my life which would be of interest – hardly to myself even now that they are parcels and portions of the survived past."

While Gogarty's children – Noll, Dermot and Brenda – were alive, they guarded their father's desire for privacy in his personal life with such determination as to make his character seem even more capricious, inconsistent and perverse. That green baize door was kept so firmly closed as to invite suspicion as to what lay behind it. A touching, if disproportionate loyalty to their father's name and reputation effectively ensured that the polymath, sometimes dubbed "renaissance man" was reduced to a silhouette.

Having lived through the civil war, their father's abduction with murderous intent and the burning of Renvyle, Gogarty's sons and daughter could be forgiven for harbouring certain inherited and extreme opinions – and they did. However, it was their reticence to divulge anything of Gogarty's private life, even decades after his death, which prompted this probe to find that elusive inner man. Professor A. Norman Jeffares provided the touch paper in his introduction to his masterly production: *The Poems & Plays of Oliver St John Gogarty.*

Gogarty kept his private life private, permitting only very rarely what we now realise are the barest hints in a few poems about his married life and fatherhood. So, no need for the bucket excavators of biographical exegis – though some water divining may be in order.

In Ireland there is an old adage: "You can take the man from the bog, but you can never take the bog from the man." It is often intended to be taken literally, to cast aspersions on those held to have risen above their station. However, it is true in a far wider sense; to wit, an individual is an ineluctable product of his or her background, imbued from infancy with inherent, fundamental values that form the core of the individual's character and endure until death. Subsequent experiences can and do effect superficial change, in part through circumstance, in part by design. Rarely does an individual contrive successfully to escape or obscure his or her origins. This is particularly true of writers, though some persist in the belief that they can divorce themselves from their writings; drawing a veil between themselves and their readers. That this is patently impossible, none knew better than Oliver St John Gogarty. Accordingly, he adopted various personae in his prose works, if not in his poetry. This stratagem ultimately redounded to his discredit.

Frustrated by what they sensed as subterfuge and exasperated by his wilful obfuscation, the critics – and his were many, eager and willing – dismissed him as a mendacious man of many masks. His political beliefs were for the most part forgiven, if not forgotten, for several reasons. In that sphere he earned the grudging respect of his enemies for his courage, consistency and conviction. Moreover, he was seen to have paid dearly for his role in the foundation of the Irish Free State, whatever it may have been. And if he later quit the field, defeated and despairing, he was not alone. That President de Valera should be said to have prorogued the Senate specifically to be rid of Gogarty and Andrew Jameson was victory enough, albeit pyrrhic.

The outcome of the celebrated libel action over *As I Was Going Down Sackville Street* allowed Gogarty's detractors to brand him anti-Semitic, as indeed he was. However, he was scarcely alone in attributing most of the economic and financial woes of the world to the machinations of "God's anointed". Moreover, Gogarty's overt anti-Semitism was – in the eyes of his detractors – incidental to his castigation of de Valera, at whose feet he repeatedly and stridently laid the blame for the civil war and the deaths of his friends and heroes, Griffith and Collins.

With the passage of time and the emergence of a cosmopolitan, materialistic Ireland, civil war politics have been all but obliterated from the national psyche. Anti-Semitism in Ireland has likewise been marginalised in the face of wholesale immigration and the spectre of a polyglot community on an island where but a few years since emigration was its economic lifeblood. It is safe to say that Oliver St John Gogarty has been forgotten for his political and racist roles.

For one to whom irony was a favourite weapon, it is perhaps the ultimate irony that his posthumous reputation should depend so disproportionately upon his portrayal in the works of another. His awareness that this might well prove to be the case underlies his curious place in the pantheon of Irish literature. For it was Gogarty's ambivalence about his depiction as "Buck Mulligan" that has tinged his own reputation with infamy. Had he been consistent in his dismissal of *Ulysses* as "a book that can be read on the lavatory walls of Dublin," his own literary output may have earned more ready acceptance, even acclaim. As it is, his wild oscillation between condemnation of Joyce and willingness to capitalise on his alter ego – Buck Mulligan – confounded his supporters and outraged his critics.

CHAPTER ONE

Margaret Oliver – "the flower of Galway" – married Dr Henry Joseph Kelly Gogarty in 1876 in Dublin, where the Meath-born fourth generation physician enjoyed a successful practice in fashionable Rutland Square East. On 17 August 1878 Margaret Gogarty gave birth in 5 Rutland Square to her firstborn. He emerged into this world with a caul on his head, a lucky portent. Sailors of that time particularly believed that possession of a baby's caul was a sure protection against death by drowning. The infant was duly christened Oliver Joseph St John Gogarty. His first and second Christian names acknowledged his father and maternal grandfather, while the distinctive St John was likely attributable to his father's desire to commemorate his late colleague and near neighbour, Dr Robert St John Mayne.

Dr Mayne had lived and practised in No 8 Rutland Square, dying in 1871 at an early age from small-pox, contracted in the Meath Hospital, where Dr Gogarty had also studied. In his biography of Oliver St John Gogarty, J. B. Lyons mooted the possibility that the Oliver St John alignment might have owed its origins to some lineal descent from an erstwhile Lord Deputy of Ireland, Oliver St John.[1]

The Gogartys had been recorded in County Meath and environs since the 11th century. As Dr MacLysaght noted in *The Surnames of Ireland*, Gogarty "is quite distinct from Fogarty though etymologically cognate." Coincidentally, the Olivers, an Anglo-Norman family, had their Irish origins in the north-east, close to the Gogartys, in neighbouring County Louth, later becoming most prominent in County Limerick in the 17th century. It was in the following century that John Wesley found a settlement of over sixty families of Palatines on the thousand-acre Oliver estate, where they had created the village of Clonodfoy under the benign protection of the colourfully named Right Honourable Sir Silver Oliver, "a most pious, judicious and amiable man". There the Palatines retained their German language and industrious way of life for over one hundred years. Castle Oliver, a red sandstone Scottish Baronial extravaganza near Kilfinane, complete with pierced "Jacobean" parapet, heraldic beasts and adjacent Oliver's Folly, was reconstructed to give employment after the famine by the Misses Oliver-Gascoigne, becoming the Oliver family seat in Ireland.[2]

As was common in Irish propertied families during the centuries of Catholic oppression in Ireland, the Olivers sailed under both pre- and post-Reformation flags, as prudence dictated. The branch from which Margaret Oliver descended was staunchly Catholic. John, her father, who had married a second time following the death of his first wife, financed the founding of a convent in Oranmore for the benefit of daughters from both of his families. Margaret's firstborn was later to take pride in his Oliver lineage.

"Fitzdominick Oliver, uncle of my grandfather, it was who seized Lord Edward Fitzgerald and dumped him into Salem. He took him from Aldingham House Galway and accused him or Wolfe Tone or one Foley of betraying him for standing in with the privateers of Brittany; and reminded him that for all his patriotism he did not hesitate to turn his guns on the women and children of Boston; for Lord Edward served in the fleet. He took Jute, an American who was spying for the British from his forecastle and strung him to the yardarm and emptied his 'gun' into him. These Fitzdominicks were of the De Burgo, now Burke, who married Granuale (Grace O'Malley) and made it possible for her to hold the Western Ocean."[3]

By aligning himself with the Olivers of Anglo-Norman lineage Gogarty eschewed much, much older Galway roots, albeit from across the mouth of the Corrib, in the Claddagh. Whereas the fortified town had been constructed within its protective walls in the twelfth century, the fishing settlement across the river mouth was thought to have existed there since at least the fifth century. The two communities did not mix or mingle, which makes it curiously coincidental that the last king of the Claddagh, who died only in 1972, should have borne the name Martin Oliver.[4]

Others born in 1878 whose lives would impact upon Gogarty's in various ways included Thomas MacDonagh, poet and revolutionary; Daniel Corkery, author of *The Hidden Ireland*; Sinead Flanagan, future wife of Eamon de Valera; Margaret Gillespie, suffragette, who married James Cousins and was to give the mendicant James Joyce a bed on the night of 15/16 June 1904 and William Orpen, society portrait painter, destined to paint both Oliver Gogarty and his son "Noll". However, one destined to prove more influential in Oliver Gogarty's life than any of these was Edward Plunkett, born less than a month earlier in Dunstall Priory in Kent. The future 18th Lord Dunsany was to become a lifelong friend.

As Oliver St John Gogarty was subsequently to reply when queried by Dr Tyrrell of TCD on his choice of profession: "It is more or less congenital in our family. Nobody ever thought of anything else for me."[5] Indeed, his great-grandfather, Henry Gogarty (1790-1853) had been a physician; his grandfather, James, had been physician to the family of Viscount Gormanston and his father had carried on the medical tradition. Born in 1842, Henry Joseph Kelly Gogarty studied medicine at the Ledwich School, becoming a Licentiate of the Royal College of Surgeons in Ireland in 1864. Two years later he became a Fellow of the RCSI and later added the Edinburgh Licentiate to his escutcheon. Having practised at 66 Blessington Street, Dr Gogarty had consolidated his rising status in both medical and social circles in Dublin by moving to the then exclusive Rutland Square in 1869.[6]

Laid out in the 1750s on three sides of Bartholomew Mosse's Lying-in Hospital, nowadays known as the Rotunda, and then the first maternity hospital in Europe, Rutland Square rapidly attracted the great and the good of pre-Act of Union Ireland in the wake of the Earl of Charlemont and Lord Wicklow. In 1752 the former, described by Edmund Burke as "the most public spirited and at the same time the best natured and best bred man in Ireland" built as his town house what is today the Dublin Municipal Gallery. Two years later Lord Wicklow conferred his seal of approval when agreeing to give £3,500 for No 4. Fashion dictated that by 1787 Rutland Square contained more resident grandees than any other Dublin location, including the considerably larger St Stephen's Green to the south of the Liffey. Five years later Rutland Square – as it was officially named in 1790 after the late Lord Lieutenant – outranked its southern rival as the most exclusive address in the "second city of the empire." One of the Wybrant family would later record that No. 47, in his family's possession from 1768 until 1884 had been, prior to the 1800 Act of Union "the only house in the square occupied by a commoner."[7]

The flight of the nobility after 1800, when Ireland's administrative autonomy effectively disappeared, left a vacuum that was speedily filled by the professions. Among the first to take advantage were Patrick Plunkett, president of the King and Queen's College of Physicians in Ireland in 1801, followed by Joseph Clarke, Master of the Rotunda Lying-in Hospital, William Gray, surgeon Ralph Smith Obre and James Cleghorn, thrice president of the K&QCPI and State Physician from 1803 until his death in 1826.

The next wave included such notables as Richard Carmichael, president RCSI, educator and reformer, who "entertained his friends hospitably and gracefully" in No. 24 from 1817 until his death in 1849. Robert Law was physician to Sir Patrick Dun's Hospital and succeeded the renowned Robert Graves as King's Professor of the Institutes of Medicine at the School of Physic of Trinity College from 1841 until 1874. Joseph Michael O'Ferrall attended Mrs Aikenhead, founder of the Irish Sisters of Charity, becoming the sole medical practitioner in St Vincent's Hospital when it was opened by the Sisters in 1834. On improving his financial circumstances, O'Ferrall consolidated a significant trend when following in Patrick Plunkett's footsteps to the increasingly fashionable Merrion Square, on the south side of the Liffey, dying there in 1868.

In 1854 Dr Henry Tweedy took up residence in No. 16, the uppermost house on Rutland Square East, forming the corner between the square and Gardiner's Row. As such it boasted twin entrances, their uses outlined by his grandson in this delightful vignette.

"The twin entrances suited Grandpa's work ideally. The Rutland Square hall-door was for his private and family use: the Gardiner's Row door was reserved for the very poor of North Dublin who consulted him in his capacity as honorary physician of the Dublin By Lamplight Society and in practice its entrance Hall was their waiting room. But it also housed an imposing coop in which Grandpa kept his bantams. They were an unfailing diversion for the patient, especially when they perched on Grandpa's shoulders."[8]

Besides his bantams Dr Tweedy kept a pet goat, which he took for its daily walk in the Rotunda Gardens. Long the senior member of his profession, Dr Tweedy met his death aged ninety-five, through falling from the ladder in his dispensary. Henry Colpoys Tweedy, his son, also a distinguished physician, had official permission to keep six sabres and a pistol in the house, reflecting concerns for his personal safety having carried out the post mortem on Sir Frederick Cavendish, assassinated in the Phoenix Park in May 1882.

Rutland Square had had more direct association with insurgence, for it was in No 22, Charlemont House, that the occupant had helped Grattan and Flood to draft the resolutions for the Volunteer Convention at Dungannon in 1780. This Lord Charlemont did in his capacity as Commander-in-chief of the Volunteers. Just a few years later Frederick Trench, consultant architect on the New Rooms adjoining the Rotunda, conveyed his concern to Lord Cornwallis that between 700 and 1,000 men were engaged in nocturnal activities in the Barley Fields to the north of Rutland Square. He anticipated a massacre if the insurgents were not denied access from the direction of Drumcondra by way of high walls and folding gates . . .

On the night of 10 December 1890 Rutland Square again featured in dispatches, as Katharine Tynan recorded: "It was nearly 8.30 pm when we heard the bands coming; then the windows were lit by the glare of a thousand torches in the streets outside. There was a distant roaring like the sea. The great gathering within waited, silent with expectation. The occasion was Charles Stewart Parnell's address to a meeting at the Rotunda." He subsequently spoke again from the balcony of No 11 – the National Club – for the benefit of the throng unable to get admission to the Rotunda meeting. Four doors up lived Dr Joseph Edward Kenny MP,

Parnell's friend, physician and frequent host. Staying there the following September, the ailing Parnell eschewed his friend's medical advice and set out for England. Six days later the "uncrowned king of Ireland" was dead.

Earlier that same year, 1891, a death much closer to home had far greater consequences for young Oliver St John Gogarty. "My father died in the same year as Parnell. I had seen crowds assembled to hear 'The Chief' speak from a house about eight doors above ours on the same side of the square. It belonged to a Dr. Kenny who must have been a friend of the Chief because it was from a balcony of his house that Parnell addressed the crowd. All are gone now, crowds and all, 'without a fame in death' except the Chief."[9] However, this is to anticipate. Much had occurred in young Oliver's life prior to the melancholy events of Saturday 7 March 1891.

CHAPTER TWO

In due course young Oliver Gogarty learned to share the nursery in 5 Rutland Square East with Mary Florence, his only sister, whose birth was registered in the 3rd quarter of 1882 by one Christina Speakman. "Mayflo" as Mary Florence was ever afterwards known, was followed into this world by Henry Arthur Hallam Devereux Gogarty, whose birth was registered by the same Christina Speakman as having occurred in 72 Upper Dominick Street on 15 November 1882.[1] Henry thus shared his birth year with three characters destined to play significant parts in this story: James Joyce, James Stephens and Eamon de Valera. The Gogarty family was completed with the birth of Richard Howard Aloysius Gogarty in Eccles Lane on 7 May 1886. As it happened, Christina Speakman did not have far to travel to register the births of the Gogarty children, for by that time Charlemont House (now the Municipal Gallery) had become the General Register and Census Office, where births and deaths were recorded.

The key to the apparent mystery of Mayflo and Henry – or Harry as he was in the family – being born within a few months of each other at most is to be found in the opening chapter of *Tumbling in the Hay*.

"Wiseman closed the door, mounted the box, and removed first an old yellow blanket from the kidneys of his mare, then from its socket an ivory whip with rounded, polished knobs, a gift from the estate of his late employer – for Wiseman was the Ouseleys' coachman in the days when there were carriages and horses in Rutland Square . . .

Wiseman's wife had been young Ouseley's wet-nurse . . .

Domestic was his bliss: he had been blessed eleven times. He was enabled, with his well-plied cab and a little help from his wife's wet-nursing (for

Providence will provide for the suckling), to rear his elevenfold family . . ."

Later on in *Tumbling in the Hay*, when writing of his mother, Gogarty makes further allusion to "Mrs Wiseman". "She could have given me a watery cow for a mother. Instead of that she suckled me and, when I asked for more, turned me on to Mrs. Wiseman – hence my teeth that can crack a Brazil nut . . ." On the assumption that "Wiseman" was in reality Speakman and on the basis that surviving photographs indicate a close proximity in age between Oliver and Mayflo, it seems reasonable to assume that Mayflo's birth was registered belatedly, its registration perhaps triggered by the imminent arrival of another sibling.

At all events, Harry's nomenclature can be attributed – in part anyway – to being christened Henry after his father and great-grandfather. Hallam remains a mystery, while the only traceable Devereux connection to be found is in the married name of Dr Henry Gogarty's niece, Emily Gordon Cumming. Similarly, Howard crops up in neither the Gogarty nor the Oliver family tree, but Richard does, as a younger brother of Dr Henry Gogarty, born in 1850. Aloysius was the professed name of one of Margaret Gogarty's sisters, a nun in California, just as it was one of the names given to a relation born to a District Inspector Gogarty, RIC, Cavan, born in 1884 and named Henry Aloysius. Mary Florence's first name clearly derived from her mother's second name, while Florence derived from Dr Gogarty's great-grandmother. Born Florence Glassford in Craig, County Meath, she had married James Gogarty, the patriarch who had lived to the remarkable age of ninety-five.[2]

Meanwhile, Dr Gogarty went about his rounds in a smart gig, with his "tiger" in liveried attendance to hold the horse while his master made his house calls. For recreation Henry Gogarty rode his hunter to and from the Phoenix Park, took shooting grounds on the Nore, shot in County Meath with his friend Farrell O'Reilly and hunted with Dick Burke, legendary Tipperary MFH. As a keen shooting man Henry Gogarty prided himself on his immaculate Irish red setters, Rufus and Garryowen, which he both shot over and showed. His eldest son would later say that it was the tedium of dying the dogs' "feather" with cold tea for dog shows that was responsible for his lifelong indifference to canines. As for shooting; any appetite he might have had was killed by his father's insistence that he should hit his quota of tin plates thrown up by Michael the manservant from behind the garden wall before he was allowed any breakfast.

The same Michael it was who greeted young Oliver on his return from school one day with news of his father's acquisition of "Fairfield", a Queen Anne house in its own extensive grounds in Glasnevin, then a village about a mile to the north of Rutland Square and still very much in the countryside. "Your father got Fairfield. Don't let on I told you anything."

Mrs Gogarty provided the requisite confirmation. "Your father's bid for Fairfield has been accepted. You will have a better place to play than in the Square." Mrs Gogarty's dislike of the Square was based on the fact that its exclusivity to householders had become a thing of the past. Gangs roamed in it, defacing all available surfaces with ribald remarks. Many years later receipt of Enid Starkey's memoirs, *A Lady's Child*, prompted Mayflo to reminisce: "all about the Dublin of our youth and the Walsh family of Rutland Square. We used to play with Mrs Hoey, etc. They all got on so well with none of the advantages we others had – except a worldly-wise mother."

The "advantages" to which Mayflo alluded were attributable to their father's status as a society physician, at that time quite an unusual achievement for a Catholic. The Dublin merchant princes of the day were almost exclusively Scottish and Presbyterian, as Alex Findlater – a surviving scion of that Scots commercial caste – related in his magnificent tome, *FINDLATERS – The Story of a Dublin Merchant Family 1774 – 2001.* John Jameson from Alloa founded his Dublin distillery in 1780. He was followed by Thomas Heiton, the coal merchant, John Arnott, of department store renown, John Boyd Dunlop, re-inventor of the pneumatic tyre, Adam Millar, wine and spirit merchant, James Mackey, seed merchant, Alexander Thom, printer, Thomas Weir, jeweller and J. B. Johnston, miller. Alexander Findlater had by this time endowed what was to become his family's monument and a Dublin landmark when financing Findlater's Church, completed on the north east corner of Rutland Square in 1864. Commerce might bind Scots Presbyterian and Irish

Catholic together, but socially they inhabited different worlds. While such distinctions meant nothing to young Oliver Gogarty at that early stage, it was a challenge and a test of character that awaited him at university.

Young Oliver began his formal education at the O'Connell Christian Brothers School, North Richmond Street. "It was no pain to go to school," as he was to write later. There the principal, Brother William A. Swann, abjured him: "chisel your words." There he first encountered Tom Kettle. "He had eyes like the eyes of Robbie Burns, the eyes of a genius." Gogarty also recalled that Tom Kettle was driven to school in a governess cart, whereas Dr Gogarty diplomatically refrained from delivering or collecting his son in his two-horse phaeton. Admittedly, young Kettle's journey to school was considerably longer than Oliver Gogarty's, for his family home was in St Margaret's. Gogarty retained affectionate memories of his first school. "I knew none of the boys well; but I did know well the propositions of Euclid and to their clear unambiguous style I owe whatever smatterings of unequivocal English I may possess." He also admired the Christian Brothers' inclusion of Irish in the curriculum, long before it became, in Gogarty's opinion, "a political Shibboleth." Some time later, as the *O'Connell School Record* reticently related in 1958.

"James A. Joyce, whose family moved from house to house, is found in 1895 living at 17 North Richmond Street. At this time, on the authority of his brother Stanislaus, they both spent a short period at O'Connell School. He refers briefly to the school and street in 'Araby', one of the short stories in *Dubliners*."

Writing over sixty years later in his "unpremeditated autobiography", Oliver Gogarty indicated that his father was no stranger to property and investment in Glasnevin. "Fairfield lay in an unfashionable neighbourhood to the north of the city on the road that went past the Botanic Gardens and the Tolka Bridge where the two tram horses rested while a third was harnessed and the climb to the tram terminus began . . . Behind St Joseph's Crescent there was a field which stretched behind Kincora Terrace and Oliver Mount, all of which my father built opposite Fairfield's boundary wall. Now, with Fairfield, he owned fields on each side of Botanic Road."

An epigram inscribed on a closet window pane was attributed to Dean Swift, as Mayflo recalled years later when writing to Oliver: "I sent today by parcel post the only photo I have of Fairfield . . . Do you remember what was engraved with a diamond on a window pane in one of the rooms?

Mary Fitzpatrick
Tender, slender very young
An ugly face but a pleasing tongue."

That inscription inspired W. B. Yeats to write his play *The Words upon the Window Pane*. Curiously, the same anecdote concerning Dean Swift's accolade to a serving girl is told of "Delville", also in Glasnevin and also a Queen Anne house. Stephen Gwynn, in his *Dublin Old & New*, glosses it thus: "Further along, before you reach the Horticultural gardens, your road passes Delville, an old and historic house, though not a great one; Swift was at the planning of it when his friend Dr. Delany decided to build here; and Dean Delany's wife wrote here many of the letters which, published long after, tell us much about the persons and manners of eighteenth-century Ireland."

Delville and its creators are also mentioned at length in *The Neighbourhood of Dublin*.

"Apart from the great cemetery by which the locality is now best known, Glasnevin is interesting chiefly by reason of the distinguished people who in bygone days made it their residence or resort. Of these perhaps the best known and most identified with the place is the celebrated divine, Dr. Delany, who lived here in the 18th century, and who assembled around the table in his charming house, Delville, all the Dublin wits and celebrities of his time. Doubtless the chief attraction to many of the visitors was the talented hostess, Mrs. Delany, to whose taste and refinement Delville owes much of its present interest. Swift and Stella were both in the habit of visiting the hospitable proprietors of Delville, and Swift wrote a squib jocosely satirising the grounds, which he considered too small for the size of the house.

The gardens are laid out to the best advantage, and retain, in their main features, the design of their originator. They contain a number of magnificent trees and shrubs, among which are arbutus, ilex and yew, many of them of venerable appearance. A pretty stream, spanned by rustic bridges, flows through the grounds which are well enclosed forming a delightful retreat, notwithstanding the rapid encroachment of the city in this direction.

A miniature temple, bearing the motto '*Fastigia despicit urbis*' (it looks down upon the pinnacles of the city), said to have been suggested by Swift, stands on a slight eminence in the grounds, and contains a medallion of Stella by Mrs. Delany."[3]

Victoria Glendinning, in her biography, *Jonathan Swift*, also refers to Dean Swift etching verse on the window pane at Delville. While two similar Queen Anne houses could conceivably have existed in Glasnevin, the conviction grew all the while that Delville and Fairfield were one and the same. Its disrepair prompted *The Irish Times* of 21 March 1942 to predict a similar fate for Delville as had recently befallen Coole Park. By the time the *Shell Guide* was published in 1962 that prediction had come true. "The nearby Bon Secours Nursing Home occupies the site of Delville, residence of Swift's celebrated friends, Dr and Mrs Delaney. For all its memorable associations and merit, the house (1729 onwards) was let fall into decay and has been recently demolished. The garden too, with its famous shell-house and temple, has been utterly destroyed."

That photograph of Fairfield that Mayflo sent to her brother may indeed be the only such likeness to have survived. At all events the Irish Architectural Archive has no pictorial record of Fairfield. However, what it does have – and in abundance – are illustrations of Delville, none of which correspond to Mayflo's photograph of Fairfield . . . Thereby was one pet theory demolished, leaving only the nagging concern that Dean Swift should have inscribed window panes in two adjacent properties.

CHAPTER THREE

Reuters Telegram from New York to Charles T. Starkey, 506 Codchaux Building, New Orleans, Sunday, 8 March, 1891:

Sudden death of Dr Gogarty

We regret to announce the death, from congestion of the liver, of Dr Henry Joseph Kelly Gogarty, which occurred rather suddenly at his residence in Rutland Square yesterday evening, about five o'clock p.m.

Though he complained of being unwell on Thursday and Friday, he was out, attending to his professional duties.

On the evening of his death he received a summons to attend a patient, and spoke to Mrs Gogarty on the subject.

Shortly afterwards he suddenly expired in the presence of his wife, who had but a few days before returned from London.

About two years ago, on his return from Paris, and again at Easter, the deceased gentleman suffered from an attack similar to that which proved fatal.

Dr Gogarty was a native of Co. Cavan and was about 49 years of age.

Death was certified by a doctor, who testified that the deceased had been ill for three days, suffering from congestion of the liver, which had brought on a syncope.[1] Annie Oliver, sister-in-law of the deceased and inmate of 5 Rutland Square, was the 'informant' of the death certificate. Only by such morbid research did the identity of Oliver Gogarty's anonymous but unquestionably influential aunt come to light. Otherwise "she who knows all about the royal family and half the *Almanach de Gotha* off by heart, and, when we have turkey, goose or gurnard for dinner, calls the stuffing 'concealment',"[2] has heretofore remained nameless, for all the times Gogarty would allude to her in his writings. Even Joyce failed to pierce the veil of Annie Oliver's anonymity in *Ulysses*: "But with the help of God and his blessed mother I'll make it my business to write a letter one of these days to his mother or his aunt or whatever she is that will open her eyes as wide as a gate. I'll tickle his catastrophe, believe you me."

The notification of Henry Gogarty's death to New Orleans proved even more revealing, as once again it shone light where Oliver Gogarty had proved consistently evasive. In this instance his defence that such detail was of no interest to his readers, since it was of no interest to him, was simply invalid. His wealth of correspondence with family members demonstrated just how keen was his interest in his American relations, on both sides of his family.

Recipients of that communication to New Orleans were the brothers Christopher and Patrick Fleming Gogarty, uncles of the deceased.[3] They had emigrated from Ireland in September 1846 – at the height of the famine. Sailing from Liverpool on 4 October, the brothers docked in Boston, Mass. on 24 November 1846. Christopher became Professor of Latin at Harvard, subsequently moving to New Orleans, where he died childless. Patrick Fleming Gogarty's movements were more precisely documented and preserved for posterity by his descendants. Thus is it known that he left Boston and arrived in New Orleans, 18 November 1853. Five years after his arrival Patrick Fleming Gogarty wed Bridget Stanley, a native of Templemore, Co Tipperary, in St John's Church, New Orleans on 6 November 1858. They had eight children, one of whom, Joseph, went on to sire an even dozen, some of whose descendants still live in New Orleans.

Others across the Atlantic to learn of Dr Henry Gogarty's untimely demise were the Olivers of New York and San Francisco, relations of Mrs Gogarty. Such information as exists on the New York branch was divulged by Bartley Oliver, San Francisco, when writing to Oliver Gogarty many years later.

"You ask about the New York Olivers. I have not seen or heard of them for years. Some of them must be alive, but the two elders, James and Francis, are dead. Jim, as he was called, was quite a politician and known as the 'King of Little Italy', left no family. Francis had quite a progeny, eight or ten . . . Next time I see Joe Oliver I will ask him. He has a wonderful memory and keeps track of the Oliver clan."[4]

Joe Oliver, a doctor in San Francisco, duly weighed in with his recollections.

"I first met your father and mother in 1878 when after a visit to your grandfather Oliver's family in Galway we spent some weeks in Dublin. I was with my father, sister Minnie and a cousin Annie Healy. Again, about two years later my father and brother-in-law Robert Tobin and I were in Ireland during the summer vacation. After my father's death in 1886, on my way to Paris, I left the boat at Queenstown to have Xmas dinner at Rutland Square . . . I was accepted as a member of the family – younger brother or elder son . . . There was a strong bond between my father and John Oliver of Galway . . . My father and mother first returned to Ireland about 1864. Father and John Oliver soon renewed acquaintance."[5]

The father in question was Dennis J. Oliver of Menlough Park, Galway. Born in 1825, Dennis Oliver was believed to have founded his fortune as one of the Forty-niners who took part in the celebrated Gold Rush of 1849. He and his brother-in-law D. C. McGlynn, also from Menlough Park, set up in San Francisco about 1850, when Dennis was listed as a wholesale dealer in paints, oils, varnishes and painters' and artists' materials. In August 1854 the brothers-in-law purchased 1,700 acres from the Governor of California and erected an arched gate bearing the inscription "Menlo Park" at the joint entrance to their two ranches. In 1863 the San Francisco and San Jose railroad reached Menlo Park, enabling Dennis Oliver to develop his land for building. The railway station opened in 1867 and seven years later Menlo Park was incorporated as a city.[6]

Young Oliver St John Gogarty, as he said himself, might have been destined by family tradition to become a physician. Nevertheless, the legacy of successful property development on both sides of his family could not but have influenced his propensity to acquire houses – even a castle – with a view to turning them over at a profit. Unfortunately, a combination of poor commercial judgement and hopeless financial management ensured that potential "goldmines" turned into loss-making liabilities. In every instance financial reverses would be attributed to the machinations and usurious practices of Jews. Gogarty's anti-Semitism, besides being widespread and overt at the time, was in his case little more than a reckless and ultimately ruinous disdain for the banking community.

Even allowing for the fact that Gogarty didn't publish his first prose – *As I Was Going Down Sackville Street* – until he was nearing fifty and his father had died when he was twelve, he had remarkably little to say about his sire. Quite clearly his childhood exposure to hunting and shooting instilled a dislike of country sports. True, he expressed a certain interest in fishing, but lacked the necessary patience to practise that art. Two anecdotes from *Tumbling in the Hay* suggest that Gogarty did not feel humour to have been his father's strongest point.

"With regard to the Hay Hotel I ought to dwell on its antecedents.

'Stephen,' said my Father, angrily it would seem, though the scene is almost forgotten, 'don't you think a man in your position is compromising Maria?' The evidence was what the lawyers call circumstantial. Stephen in dishonour stood and muttered something. 'You will both leave my employment in the morning.' Thus it came about that Maria, the cook, who was so skilled at making those entrées called *Madeleines en surprise*, owed her exit to her entrée, or rather to her being taken *en surprise* in the house. I always felt proud when I heard that almost unremembered act of love recounted, that my Father did not ask, 'What are you two doing?' It would have been banal, and, coming from a doctor, not to be excused.

So they retired to the mews and acquired the premises which, from the load of hay constantly replenished in one of its windows for the refreshment of night-weary cab-horses, was called the Hay Hotel."

The other reference to his father, indicating a grave disposition, occurs in the same book, when Golly desperately seeks a virility potion, having just remarried.

"Then, just to show these merchants' sons that there was medicine in the blood, 'My father,' I said solemnly, 'on one occasion prescribed mulled Burgundy, a dozen oysters and a mattress in front of the fire. 'And if that fails,' asked the patient, 'what will I do then?' 'Then send for me.' I don't suppose my father, who was a serious man, saw the joke."

There remains one other, enigmatic reference by Gogarty to his father, contained in *It Isn't This Time of Year at All!*, when he reflects on the violent death of O'Leary, the ringleader of the gang that had kidnapped him from his house in Ely Place, with every intention of shooting him. "I felt normal again. It was said of my father that his enemies all came to a bad end. I had taken after him." That cryptic observation begs a question. Why should a Dublin physician have aroused enmity, hardly in his principal profession? Hunting and shooting can and do give rise to healthy sporting rivalry, but rarely to antagonism. In the absence of any known political activity, property development remains the prime suspect. Gogarty's abiding interest in property and its potential would suggest as much.

CHAPTER FOUR

In 1890 young Oliver Gogarty transferred schools, exchanging the Christian Brothers and the O'Connell School for the Jesuits in Belvedere, around the corner from Rutland Square East, in what is now Great Denmark Street. Belvedere College was founded in the town house of George Rochfort, second Earl of Belvedere, for whom it was built in 1775, following its purchase by the Society of Jesus in 1841. Its popularity in time necessitated expansion and in 1884 the Jesuits acquired the adjoining house, formerly belonging to Lord Fingall. In all likelihood he would have completed his secondary education at Belvedere, living at home, as a prelude to enrolling in Trinity College, like his father before him. However, his father's sudden death, aged forty-nine and intestate, had immediate and profound consequences for his eldest son. While Mrs Gogarty continued to maintain both No 5 Rutland Square and Fairfield, she was able to do so only by flouting the law and taking the administration of her late husband's estate into her own hands.[1] By virtue of Dr Gogarty dying without having executed a valid will, his estate should, legally, have gone into Chancery.

An additional factor in young Oliver's abrupt change of regime may have been his natural boisterousness, which he would later attribute to his mother. "It is to her that I owe that extra energy which unfortunately makes it so difficult for me to sit long in one place if there is a textbook in the vicinity and not a barrel."[2] Mayflo, who provided the biographer Ulick O'Connor with invaluable childhood recollections of life in 5 Rutland Square, related how Oliver, in response to his mother's strictures about being present for daily prayers, hit upon the idea of putting whiskey in the cats' milk. The intoxicated felines reacted by rocketing up and down the stairs, wailing like demented banshees. Mayflo also recounted the stratagem evolved by Oliver and Harry to atone for various demeanours. They took up position, back to back, heads touching, behind their mother's chair before breakfast. When the lady of the house was seated they began quoting, alternately, from a dedication to Mrs Gogarty in *Letters of an Irish Catholic Layman*, by "old Keating, who was the father of two Jesuits."[3] The inscription read: "To Mrs. Margaret Gogarty, a lady whom, to all the graces and attractions of her sex, adds virile force of intellect and judgement, this little book is respectfully dedicated by the author." Understandably, the recitation of such an encomium invariably achieved forgiveness.

Such reprieves were but temporary, for Mrs Gogarty responded to the prospectus for Mungret College, "situated on a gentle eminence rising from the Shannon". Her eldest son was more prosaic.

"I was sent to a third-rate boarding school . . . My brother never went to such a school, and now he is much taller than I. I was stunted; no wonder I am but five foot nine. I was starved; undernourished in body and soul at a most susceptible age . . . I became so emaciated after a few months that I was not sent back but was bundled off to England where the routine was the same, but the food was somewhat better and the school was cleaner."[4]

As J. B. Lyons was to observe in his biography of Gogarty, it seemed scarcely credible that such an exuberant and outgoing youth should find boarding school so oppressive. Many years after his release from Stonyhurst, Gogarty was to write: "That school was the scene of so much unhappiness that I accepted unhappiness as the norm! I have never mentioned it to anyone. It is amazing how you heard of it: Stonyhurst the Accurst."[5] Gogarty was less than accurate in saying that he had never referred to Stonyhurst, even if he did not name the school. For in his "unpremeditated autobiography" he alluded plainly to it.

"I never complained, for I imagined that no school could be otherwise, and that all schools were miserably similar. It seemed I was right when I read about the Eton of fifty years ago. Yet Protestant schools as a rule were better. For one thing, they taught better; any 'public school' boy could outwrite us in Latin verses by fifty to one. We were taught to compose Latin verses like jigsaw puzzles, irrespective of ear.[6]

"Maybe I was 'hard to handle'. That I will concede. I will concede, too, that teaching such as me was no pleasant task. Nevertheless, traffic with the lads in black made life so uncertain it seemed fruitless to learn.

"They nearly took the mercury out of me. I will be fair; it may have been fifty-fifty, a 'fair shake'; but they should have known better than to expect anyone to learn that which the teacher hates. It gave me pleasure to underline in my translation of Plato; 'knowledge which is acquired under compulsion obtains no hold on the mind.' When I think of the uncomplaining and unquestioning way I suffered in two of my three boarding schools I know that I was docile, and a fool. I had done nothing to be treated as a criminal is treated, with dislike, suspicion and distrust. Walking in Indian file along the wall, which we had to do in each corridor! What was that for but to make you feel servile? Well, the sons of wealthier parents than my widowed mother had to submit to that treatment. When I got to understand it afterwards I realized that all this hardship was intended to wean boys from their homes. Homesickness was part of the discipline. The school instead of the home.

"I was experiencing a medieval discipline, the rule of some fourteenth-century monastery on the Continent. The Middle Ages were about us with their fears, discomforts and their superstitions. Though it was in England, it could not be called an English school. It was a religious jail. There must be something resilient or devil-may-care in me that saved me from becoming embittered and resentful for the rest of my life. The only result was a recoil from all they practised. I was thinking all the more of getting out from all that was going on within. In spite of three grave accidents I was saved by the gymnasium, the swimming pool and the playing fields. And, I must add, the pride I felt each time I saw my straight young brother walk down to the dais to take a prize."[7]

For all Gogarty's dislike of the Jansenist regime that prevailed in Stonyhurst, he did manage to acquire and retain sufficient knowledge "under duress" to pass the matriculation exam, thereby obtaining a place in the Royal University of Ireland in the summer of 1896. His attitude to Stonyhurst could hardly have been improved by being left there one Christmas because his mother could not bring him home for the holidays. Instead, he contacted Preston Soccer Club and turned out for their reserve at thirty shillings a week, and this at a time when professional sports players were discriminated against, even to the extent of entering and leaving the field by separate entrances to the socially elitist "gentlemen" players.[8] That took courage, particularly for a public school boy. While Gogarty never attributed his difficulties in Stonyhurst to his being Irish, his accent and manner of speech must have marked him apart in an environment where conformity was all-important. Any perusal of *Punch* cartoons of the day prove the point; 'Paddy' was a figure of fun; an object of derision.

Over sixty years later Gogarty's grandson was to encounter similar sectarian sentiment in a sister Jesuit public school just down the Thames from Eton. Beaumont College was founded in 1861 and soon afterwards issued a sporting challenge to Eton. Back came the disdainful response: "What is Beaumont?" The Jesuits were incensed: "Beaumont is what Eton was, a school for the sons of English Catholic gentlemen!" The relevance of this anecdote lies in the strategic inclusion of the word "English". That atmosphere of jingoism and outright xenophobia prevailed in English public schools until recent times. Indeed, such petty discrimination was not exclusively reserved for 'Johnny foreigner'. It has long been held, with every justification, that it only takes one Englishman to open his mouth for another to condemn him.

While Oliver St John Gogarty had achieved his primary objective – admission to the Royal University of Ireland – he was too young to be allowed the freedom of an undergraduate, or so his mother and his influential Aunt Annie decided. In any case, it was not uncommon at that time for students to take First Arts while still safely ensconced in school. Mrs Gogarty, being an ardent Catholic, further believed that the Royal University was a safer seat of learning for her firstborn than Trinity College, notwithstanding that her late husband had defied Catholic convention in going there. As that embargo on Irish Catholics attending Trinity – later upon pain of excommunication – continued right through the reign of

Archbishop McQuaid (retired 1972), Mrs Gogarty's preference is easily understood. That the Royal University – by then the vestiges of Newman's University – was little more than an examining board with only a few small colleges seems to have counted for little in 5 Rutland Square.

Gogarty's intervening year was spent at Clongowes Wood College, another Jesuit academy, near the village of Clane in County Kildare and long since renowned as one of the foremost public schools in Ireland. As a property it first appeared in a Roll of Henry IV, dated 24 February 1417, whereby one third of the "Sylva de Clongow" was assigned as part of the dowry of Anastasia Wogan of Rathcoffey. The estate later passed into the possession of the acquisitive Anglo-Norman family Fitz-Eustace. Their decision to side with the Irish in the uprising of 1641 cost them their lands, and also the life of nonagenarian Mrs Eustace, murdered by the occupying royalist garrison for her refusal to surrender the key to a stronghold within the castle. That doughty old lady concealed the key in her mouth. In breaking her jaws to secure the key, the soldiery killed her.

The confiscated estate was bought by Sir Richard Reynell, who sold it in 1667 to the Browne family, who re-christened the property Castlebrowne. Through inter-marriage with the Wogans of Rathcoffey the owners became Wogan-Brownes. It was Thomas Wogan-Browne who in 1788 and to his own design created the present Gothic Revival building that is the centrepiece of Clongowes today. Many of the family went on to earn renown in the armies of Europe. General Michael Wogan-Browne of the Saxon Army fought under Napoleon in the Grand Army that besieged Moscow. In his absence Castlebrowne was administered by his sisters. The ladies were dutifully engaged in needlework one day when the servants downstairs were suddenly petrified by the appearance in the hallway of an officer clutching his breast from which blood flowed, staining his white uniform crimson. The gory apparition ascended the stairs, heading for the room where the ladies sat tatting . . . When concern for their mistresses overcame their fear, the servants followed in the intruder's footsteps. While the Misses Wogan-Browne claimed to have seen nothing, they instantly concluded that their brother had fallen in battle on some foreign field and immediately ordered Masses, mourning and even a wake. Two weeks later they received the doleful confirmation that General Wogan-Browne had been killed in action at the battle of Prague, at the precise time that his ghost had appeared in his ancestral home.

In the circumstances the stricken general might have been excused his oversight. Castlebrowne was no longer his property. Having inherited in 1810, he discovered to his dismay that the property was hopelessly encumbered, far beyond his capacity to redeem. Deciding to continue his military career rather than grapple with the repressive anti-Catholic laws that then prevailed in his native land, the general had sold Castlebrowne to the Irish Jesuits in 1813. They, in their turn, had to overcome strenuous government opposition before opening Clongowes Wood as a public school.

Here Oliver St John Gogarty was one of just three First Arts students, the others being Hugo V. Flinn and James N. Meenan.[9] Clongowes was to prove a delightful contrast to the rigours of Stonyhurst.

"When I returned to Ireland I had to mark time before I would be old enough to join a medical school. So I was sent to another boarding school. The best of the lot. There I met Tom Kettle again. He was about fifteen and as big as the biggest boy and his limbs were longer and better boned than most. Under a low broad forehead, which a lock of hair made lower, glowed those dark eyes of his which held always a playful smile. His restlessness revealed his courageous, liberal and unchained soul. His was the terse and graphic phrase. I remember his description of a racing cyclist entering the straight and preparing to go all out: 'he put down his head.' There comes under my eyelid a moving picture of his gray-clad figure scorching round the gravel cycling track of the school, his long legs pushing power into the pedals, his brown face bright with exercise, and a glow in his dark eyes that could light a room.

"Though I was two years older I took to imitating him. I am easily influenced by those I admire. His honesty and enthusiasm could have influenced one less susceptible than I. The successes of his older brother Andy on the cycling track added to Tom's glory.

"Very few had bicycles at our school. I got one for a present; and I got my heart's desire. Though it was a roadster I converted it, as much as such a heavy machine could be converted, into the semblance of a racing bicycle. The transformation was effected by lowering the handlebars, changing the saddle and removing the guard that covered the chain. I imagined myself equipped for racing, though the amount of road work that poor bicycle had to do would have worn out any racing model. I thought nothing of riding thirty miles a day to play football for the Bohemians in Dublin, and the same distance back after dark. I took no credit for this performance, for it caused no fatigue; but I regretted every mile that was not on the racing track because it detracted from the raciness of my machine.

"The school authorities let me out so that I might decant my energy, lest it burst the staves. In summer I played cricket on the First Eleven. The only thing I can remember is that I bowled out Captain Bonham-Carter of the garrison with the first ball. All in all I enjoyed this school, which was a great relief from my English education. They fed us well. They did not try to break your will and leave you spineless. There were fine trees about the place; and there was the Liffey, black and bright; and one of the prefects came from an old Galway family well known for their eccentricities, the mad Dalys. James Augustine Joyce was at the same school but, as he was four years younger, he was in a different grade, so I did not meet him there. It was not until later years, when we were at the Royal University, that we met. Then 'we two were nursed upon the selfsame hill', as Milton called the plain of Cambridge."[10]

The restlessness that he so admired in Tom Kettle, combined with an element of personal modesty, impelled Gogarty to condense his year at Clongowes into three paragraphs. That same restlessness and impatience infused his speech and even more so his writing. "*Carpe diem*" might have been his catchword. It remained to his biographers to unearth and record the exploits that gained Gogarty the reputation as the most outstanding Clongownian in many a long year.

It was in January 1897 that Clongowes challenged the might of Bohemians, the top amateur soccer team in Dublin. After a scoreless first half the senior men gradually wore down the schoolboys to win by three goals to one, that being scored by Oliver Gogarty. The Bohemians' selectors were sufficiently impressed to invite Gogarty and O'Shaugnessy from the Clongowes XI to play for them against Belfast's Cliftonville. Gogarty became a regular member of the team, winning a coveted gold medal when Bohemians triumphed in that season's cup final.[11] Whereas Bohemians appear to have turned a blind eye to young Gogarty's having compromised his amateur status by playing for Preston for a wage, Trinity would later adopt a more inflexible attitude.

Turning his hand to cricket with equal facility, Oliver Gogarty was the hero of the Clongowes side in their defeat of the Dublin Garrison. Besides removing the garrison's crack batsman, Captain Bonham Carter, with his first ball, he took three further wickets for only sixteen runs. His emulation of Tom Kettle on the cycling track paid dividends with a memorable victory over his exemplar in the three-mile race at the school sports day on Easter Sunday. At an infinitely more important level Oliver Gogarty rescued a man from drowning in the Liffey in Clane and prevented a fellow student from choking to death in the school refectory by whipping a fishbone out of the boy's gullet with his finger as masters and boys looked on helplessly. J. J. Horgan, a contemporary at Clongowes, subsequently recalled Oliver Gogarty as "the most popular boy in the school with his soft voice, witty tongue, and pallid handsome face." It was from the same source that Ulick O'Connor learned of Gogarty's earliest recorded poetry. It took the form of a rhyming and blatantly blasphemous account of a cricket match between Heaven and Hell, which would have consigned its author to the lower of those estates in the eyes of his mentors had his identity become known. At a more conventional level Gogarty had a poem published in the 1897 edition of *The Clongownian*.

Between sporting exploits and humanitarian achievements Oliver Gogarty found enough time to apply himself to the more mundane business of passing his First University Examination, as indeed did Hugo Flinn and James Meenan. His marks were moderate but sufficient to achieve his eventual graduation from boarding school to the exciting world of the university student. Having caused him abject misery at their hands in Stonyhurst, the Jesuits made him ample amends at Clongowes. Even so, it was apparently a case of too little, too late. Gogarty's two sons would be educated by the Benedictines, at Downside.

Later still Gogarty's attitude to his mentors underwent another change. Among his contemporaries at Clongowes had been one Daniel E. Williams, son of the Tullamore distiller of the same name and creator of 'Tullamore Dew'. In time Brenda, Gogarty's only daughter, would marry Desmond, son of Gogarty's contemporary at Clongowes. When the question arose as to where their son should go to school, Gogarty sided with his son-in-law in favouring Beaumont – another Jesuit institution – over Downside, while also warning of the horrors of Stonyhurst. It was enough to strike fear into the heart of any youngster.

Oliver St John Gogarty had just turned eighteen when he entered Clongowes down that long, potentially daunting avenue on 1 September 1896, already a veteran of two boarding schools and sometime professional footballer. Clongowes Wood and its complement of "boys in black" held little fears for such a mature student. How very different Clongowes must have seemed to James Joyce, enrolled there by his doting father, John Stanislaus Joyce, in September 1888, before he was quite seven years of age. As the Joyces were then living in Bray, the French College of the Holy Ghost Fathers in nearby Blackrock might have been more convenient and certainly more nationalist in philosophy, but the O'Connell association with Clongowes determined John Stanislaus's choice. Daniel O'Connell had sent his sons there, while John and Charles O'Connell and another relation, John Daly from Cork, had also been entrusted to the Jesuits. And the Jesuits, in John Stanislaus's estimation, were gentlemen.

May Joyce shed tears at parting with her eldest, hardly more than an infant in her eyes, even if she had been delivered of four more children in the interim and was pregnant yet again. His ebullient father merely gave young James two five-shilling pieces, told him never to inform on another boy and left him to his fate. Taking pity on the boy because of his tender years, Father John Conmee, the rector, allowed him to sleep in the infirmary, rather than have him subjected to the rigours of a dormitory.

Joyce overcame his traumatic introduction to boarding school to the extent that he had gained the respect of peers and superiors alike when either prolonged illness or his father's increasingly precarious finances saw young Jim removed from Clongowes in October 1891. While the precise date is unknown, Joyce was to place himself in Clongowes at the time of Parnell's death – 6 October.[12] For all his anti-clericalism Joyce remained adamant that his education at the hands of the Jesuits in Clongowes stood to him for the rest of his life. His association with the "Soldiers of Christ" resumed when Father Conmee, who had moved from Clongowes to Belvedere, offered to have James Joyce and his brothers educated there, free of charge. In the meantime James and his brother Stanislaus had attended the O'Connell School in North Richmond Street, despite their father's vocal misgivings at exposing his offspring to the influence of the Christian Brothers.[13]

Was it a portent of things to come that Gogarty and Joyce should have attended three schools in common, but in a contradictory sequence? Gogarty had progressed from the Christian Brothers and their O'Connell School, through the Jesuits at Belvedere and ultimately at Clongowes. Joyce's scholastic career commenced in Clongowes, continued at the O'Connell School and concluded at Belvedere. Gogarty had received additional exposure to Jesuit teaching at both Mungret and Stonyhurst. Whereas Gogarty remained firm in his praise for the foundation he obtained from the Christian Brothers, Joyce was to echo his father's disregard for that order – "Paddy Stink and Micky Mud" – preferring to consider the Jesuits the gentlemen of Catholic education. Empathising with his subject, Richard Ellmann claimed that James Joyce never alluded to his time with the Christian Brothers in his writings. The O'Connell School Union record of 1958 held differently, observing that Joyce made reference to both the school and the street in 'Araby', one of the stories in *Dubliners*.

CHAPTER FIVE

Gogarty's career on leaving Clongowes has proved a difficult trail to decipher. In a later life he would exult in laying false trails, particularly in America, where his correspondence reveals what was tantamount to a fixation about misleading callers, casual enquirers and correspondents. He seemed to take an irrational glee in purporting to visit one place, while already determined to be in another. So it was with his early days as an undergraduate. As Buck Mulligan, Gogarty is portrayed as mercurial – itself a play on words – whereas perverse is possibly more appropriate.

Whereas Ulick O'Connor records that Mrs Gogarty entered her son at the Royal University to study medicine, J. B. Lyons reveals that Oliver St John Gogarty's name is to be found in the Trinity College *Entrance Book*, 5 July 1897. At all events he would appear to have studied second year Arts under the auspices of the Royal until the summer of 1898, when he failed Second Arts in all subjects. By O'Connor's account Gogarty spent two years at the Royal, cycling during the day with the Irish champion, Charles Pease, and carousing at night. Of the ten examinations he sat for the Royal he passed just two. In *Tumbling in the Hay* Gogarty ascribes his abrupt transfer from the Cecilia Street medical school (affiliated to the Royal) to Trinity. Perhaps remembering that early advice to "chisel your words", he left a more cryptic account of that momentous decision in his "unpremeditated autobiography", *It Isn't This Time of Year at All!*

"Doctoring was in our family, so off to see Dr Bermingham my mother took me. He was registrar of the Catholic University Medical School. His want of manners was so evident that, at the end of the interview, when he pattered out: 'Here's a pamphlet in which you will find the answers to all your questions', holding out the pamphlet as he kept on writing, there was no one to take the extended brochure. I was driven out of Cecilia Street, up Dame Street, to be entered in Trinity College!

"There, the registrar was Dr Traill, afterwards Provost. Though he hailed from the North of Ireland his brusqueness did not make him rude. He was considerate of others, and therefore a gentleman. He won my mother's approval at once because he asked, 'Won't you be seated? And may I ask if you are related to my friend the late Dr Henry Gogarty?' After that it was Faire and Softly. As we drove away my mother said: 'Now that you are entered among gentlemen I hope you will never forget to behave like one.' A large order among the wild medicos of those days! A hope that could not be fulfilled if I had to satisfy my aunt, who had not only the *Almanach de Gotha* by heart but *Burke's Landed Gentry* as well. Yet it must have gone hard with my mother to enter me in a Protestant university. The fact that it had been my father's intention to do so may have consoled her; and it was not then a matter of excommunication to enter Trinity."

That observation contains a double irony, for it was not in fact until 1793 that Trinity College Dublin admitted Catholics to its degrees and subsequently to all her faculties. Instituted in the reign of Elizabeth I, Trinity was intended to be the *Mater Universitatis* with many colleges, but, like Aaron's serpent rod, it swallowed up the other halls and, as Harvard was later to do, imposed its laws and even its name on the whole University. The austerity of Trinity's academic regime extended to a ban on marriage for the Provost and the Fellows, as Charles Graves reminded his readers in *Ireland Revisited*. "The Provost and the Fellows of Trinity could not be legally married until Queen Victoria ascended the throne. Yet they were constantly breaking the law, to the great scandal of the University, and my grandfather knew several Senior Fellows whose wives were introduced by their maiden names. However, two or three bachelor Fellows, my grandfather amongst them, got a Memorial signed by the heads of the University, and very appropriately presented it to the Queen about the time of her own marriage, asking for the abolition of the Celibacy Statute, a petition which she graciously granted." [1]

While Gogarty would later describe his time at the Royal as a waste in academic terms, he did appreciate making the acquaintance of such as John Elwood, Vincent Cosgrave, Francis Sheehy Skeffington, Simon Broderick – and James Joyce. The last-named, who entered University College in the autumn of 1898, took the same tram home as Gogarty and thus they struck up a friendship, at least by Gogarty's account. Joyce would later portray them as meeting in the reading room of the National Library in Kildare Street. Gogarty was by then almost twenty and Joyce more than three years his junior. However, what would appear a significant disparity in years at their respective ages may well have been lessened to a huge degree by their contrasting backgrounds. For all his sporting exploits Gogarty had experienced a very sheltered upbringing, closeted in boarding schools – largely in the isolated wilds of Lancashire – since his father's untimely death in 1891, when he had been only twelve. Even as he approached his majority he remained very much under his mother's thumb. Mrs Gogarty, for her part, would seem to have deferred at every turn to her sister's wishes in respect of young Oliver's development.

James Augustine Joyce came from radically different circumstances. His proud but improvident father had squandered his inheritance, sired an unsupportable number of children, broken his wife's health and failed to hold down any form of regular employment. Quite apart from financial mismanagement, John Stanislaus Joyce had paid the price for being an ardent and vociferous supporter of Charles Stewart Parnell, former "uncrowned king of Ireland", by then both dead and in enduring disgrace. John Stanislaus continued to rail against the injustices he had to endure, while moving from house to house as the rent fell into arrears. James, his eldest living child, had long since learned the skills and subterfuges necessary for survival. He was in modern parlance "streetwise". Moreover, he was sufficiently intelligent to realise that his family's frequent changes of abode were never for the better and could not be offset by the invariable prominence accorded to family portraits, hastily hung in pride of place to convey the illusion of the Joyces' standing in society.

Young James Joyce's inherited traits also included an abiding conviction that the world owed him a living. While neither his father nor his grandfather had done anything to sustain – much less augment – the family fortunes, they firmly believed that connections existed to be used to their advantage, without any corresponding obligation on their part to acknowledge or repay any favours so obtained. Friends, acquaintances and relatives were all fair game. Enormous emphasis was placed on the Joyces' connection to Daniel O'Connell, through John Stanislaus's mother, Ellen O'Connell. The particulars of consanguinity with 'The Liberator' were a trifle vague. However, Ellen's recollections of Ireland's most celebrated son calling on her grandfather, Charles O'Connell, during his annual visits to Cork for the Assizes were held to be proof enough of their kinship. Daniel O'Connell's appointment as Lord Mayor of Dublin in 1841 represented a major breakthrough for Catholics in Irish politics.

A decade later Peter Paul McSwiney, another of the Joyces' relations, left his native Cork to seek his fortune in Dublin, where he opened his New Mart in Sackville Street, opposite the General Post Office. That inspired move was prompted by the imminent International Exhibition of 1853. McSwiney's commercial success was to see him become Lord Mayor of Dublin in 1865. In that capacity Peter Paul had the honour of laying the foundation stone for the monument in Sackville Street to his distinguished kinsman, Daniel O'Connell. Thus was born the Joyce family catch-phrase "my cousin Peter Paul McSwiney," utilised at every opportunity by James Joyce's grandfather, who died in 1866, and by his son John Stanislaus to enhance their family's standing by association. That association was brought into play either as endorsement or veiled threat, as appropriate. Cadging had become an inherent Joyce family failing, one the youthful James would never surmount.

Peter Paul McSwiney's decision to become involved in whiskey distilling had brought John Stanislaus Joyce up from Cork to the capital, where he became secretary of the newly created Dublin & Chapelizod Distillery Company, holding that position from 1873 until 1876, when the company went into voluntary liquidation. During the intervening decades John Stanislaus had been variously an accountant, secretary of the United Liberal Club, rate collector and advertising salesman. And all the while his once-considerable inheritance dwindled steadily to nothing, other than his cherished family portraits.

There was another perceived difference between this unlikely pair, united in their love of Elizabethan literature and lyrics, bawdy verse and general iconoclasm. Oliver St John Gogarty fancied himself as about to inherit a substantial property portfolio, amassed by his father, on turning twenty-one. It was merely a matter of time. James Joyce laboured under no such delusion. He would have to live on his wits. If friendship with Gogarty should necessitate swallowing his pride and enduring the shafts of Gogarty's mordant wit, it was a price worth paying. Moreover, all doors appeared to open to Gogarty, an assiduous collector of people, with consequent advantage for his less fortunate, less extrovert acquaintances.

Although Gogarty may have affected to patronise his younger friend, he could not help but admire Joyce's passion for language, literature and learning, around which his life had already begun to revolve to the exclusion of virtually all else, save the necessity to keep body and soul together. Conscious of his own remarkable capacity to read and memorise verse, Gogarty recognised that in this respect Joyce was indeed his equal. United in their love of the written and spoken word, the two young men differed in their intentions. Gogarty would versify for amusement, academic kudos and occasional monetary reward. Joyce saw Shakespeare as his benchmark in his quest to revolutionise English literature. Such singular focus was alien to Gogarty's sunny, self-confident appetite for life in all its guises.

Gogarty the irreverent undergraduate might not have overtly courted publicity, but he seemed destined to attract it from his earliest days in the big, bad, exciting outside world. *The Clongownian*, June 1898, carried the following account.

"Clongownians, of the last few years in particular, will have read with no little pleasure and pride the account of the gallant rescue by Oliver Gogarty of an unfortunate man who had fallen into the Liffey. It appears that Oliver was passing over Butt Bridge on his bicycle, when his attention was attracted by a large crowd. On going to the edge of the Quay, he perceived a man struggling in the water, and without a moment's delay he plunged in to his assistance. Encumbered as he was with his clothes he had much difficulty in keeping the drowning man afloat, and probably would have lost his own life, had not one of the bystanders jumped in to his assistance with a lifebuoy and all three were brought safely to land. We trust that Oliver's plucky action will be properly recognized in the proper quarter, but in the meanwhile we congratulate our late school-fellow on the courage he displayed when so many others held back."

Over half a century later J. F. Byrne, friend and confidante of James Joyce during their early years in Dublin, broke his lifelong silence on those days and published his autobiography: *Silent Years – An Autobiography with Memoirs of James Joyce and Our Ireland*. Such was the excitement in the publisher's offices, Frank O'Connor cautioned the editor, "Don't tell the Joyce experts. They will tear you apart, and tear the book away from you." His concern was understandable, for John Francis Byrne was none other than "Cranly" in *Ulysses* and he had vanished from the scene since emigrating to New York in 1910. In one chapter Byrne alludes to Joyce's prowess as a swimmer, in contrast to his own fear of water, stemming from having twice loss consciousness while trying to master "natatory skill". Then follows this graphic vignette.

"I remember one afternoon watching with almost envious admiration a youth effecting the courageous and skillful rescue of a sturdy man who was attempting suicide in Anna Liffey, just a few yards west of Butt Bridge. This young rescuer had left his bicycle, with his coat thrown on it, on the footpath beside the Liffey wall; and I stood there admiring the way he lugged his reluctant and recalcitrant freight to the foot of a flight of steps, where he, the freight, was lifted out of the water and attended to by a few men, including a bobby. The young rescuer, seeing that his charge was apparently in good hands, ran nimbly up the steps and came to retrieve his coat and bicycle; and then, having put his coat on over his dripping shirt, he immediately jumped on his bicycle, turned into Hawkins Street, and sped away without a word to anyone. This young man had done a deed which was triply courageous: first in jumping into the Liffey at a time and place where the current was swift and treacherous, second in tackling a would-be suicide, and third in plunging into a stretch of water which, at that time, was just a cesspool. Indeed, when he came up out of it his face was smeared with filth, and black muck dripping from his clothes. I was scarcely able to recognise him as the customarily spruce, well-groomed, and debonair Oliver St John Gogarty."

Trinity College at the end of the nineteenth century was at the height of its powers, its distinguished alumni including such as Jonathan Swift, Oliver Goldsmith, Edmund Burke, Oscar Wilde and John Millington Synge, to name but a few, and those selected exclusively from one field of endeavour. TCD was also held to have the finest medical faculty in Europe. As such it should have been an earthly paradise for the medical student with literary leanings. That hardly proved to be the case in the instance of Oliver St John Gogarty. He showed more interest in cycling and the revival of Irish culture, a movement initiated by Douglas Hyde, one day to become the first President of Ireland.

Once again *The Clongownian* was proud to trumpet the cycling success of its colourful past pupil, as it did in the Christmas issue of 1899.

"Mr Oliver St John Gogarty . . . was while at college a cyclist of no mean merit and has since come to the front at the sport in Ireland. Last season some of the best prizes fell to him, and he won altogether eleven first places, besides several seconds. His time for the 20 miles Championship of Ireland was 52 mins., 3⁴/₅ sec., a record for the event. He also defeated J. McBourke and L. R. Oswald in a ten miles scratch race in London and at home won the mile and five miles handicaps of TCD, starting from the scratch mark. For the former race he obtained the only standard medal which has been given for several years. Other successes fell to Mr Gogarty at Ballsbridge, Kilkenny and Dundalk; while in the competition between the Universities of Dublin and Oxford he took a second place, as he did also at the mile championship of Trinity College and the three miles championship of Ireland."

The *Irish Wheelman* described Gogarty as "an athlete who is really a sprinter, but who by assiduous training has learned to stay." His 20-

mile time, a record, was to stand for many years, while his victims over shorter distances, Isodore MacBourke and Larry Oswald, were English and Irish champions respectively. Robert Reynolds, third in the world mile championship in Copenhagen, recalled Gogarty as "a first rate cyclist. You had to watch him like a hawk in a race. If you took your eyes off him for a second he was past in a flash, with his cry 'Up, up Balrothery.' You see we trained on Balrothery Straight."[2]

Charlie Pease had played a crucial role in enabling Gogarty to set the 20-mile record, over a course in the Phoenix Park. The record-breaker invoked Pease's aid in the aftermath, as he recounted in his "unpremeditated autobiography".

"At breakfast my mother saw it as she turned over *The Irish Times*. Inwardly she may have been proud but she certainly concealed it. 'Your professors in Dublin University will hardly find your exploit a matter for congratulation. If you must indulge in athletics, why not play cricket for the university, or join the Rowing Club?' If cycling appeared to her to be an ignoble pastime, the silence in which I received her rebuke was most noble. I was about to say, 'Don't I play football for them?' But I remembered how I played against them for my old club, the Bohemians, and the disparaging remarks in the weekly paper, *T.C.D.*: 'His game is that of a professional.'

"Until I brought the conversation round to Charlie Pease I could not rest. I made it clear that he was a member of the Al Fresco Club and that he came from a distinguished Yorkshire family, one member of which, Sir Something Pease, was a member of Parliament. 'If your friend is a member of that family, he must be of a cadet branch, very cadet,' my aunt remarked. Then to soften it she said, 'God has blessed you with a robust body. Youth must find an outlet for its energy. If you can spare the time from your studies, you might join the Ward Union Hunt.' The stockbrokers, barristers, wheel-chair stag hunters – Saturdays only!"

Besides cycling Gogarty found himself lifesaving again in 1899, having earlier received the Royal Humane Society's bronze medal "for having saved life from drowning," as previously recorded. On this occasion he went to the rescue of a Mr John Meeke, who got into difficulties in the sea off Balbriggan. Tragically, this attempt proved unsuccessful, owing to others' inept handling of the rescue boat. Perhaps it was inevitable that his medical studies suffered in the face of so much distraction. Having passed in botany and zoology in the autumn of 1898, Oliver Gogarty did not confront his examiners for a further three years; a leisurely progress, even by the standards of the time. While he was never to indicate as much in his "unpremeditated autobiography", Gogarty's cavalier approach to medical school and the business of graduation may not have been unconnected to his expectations of inheritance. Why otherwise did a professional qualification occupy such a lowly place in his priorities?

Gogarty continued his winning ways on the tracks of Ireland throughout the 1900 season, winning the scratch mile in the College races, in addition to the mile and the five-mile double at the RIC sports at Ballsbridge. Inevitably there were spills, as he recalled.

"I had been skinned once or twice in my time, and had to spend nights with my knees in band-boxes to keep the clothes off, and wear gloves to hide my hands, and stay away from meals. That's the reason I have white shiny knee-caps now, for Ballsbridge has nice clean sand. My blue elbows came from cinders at Jones's Road." Nor was competition on the track the only danger Gogarty faced, for he had broken the mould as a Trinity undergraduate in taking part in open events. His greatest fear was that his formidable aunt should see his name on posters all over Dublin, advertising his participation against all-comers. "For the rest, were they not all tradesmen? Could I point to one, with the exceptions mentioned [Charlie Pease, Larry Oswald and Alfred E. Reynolds] who was not engaged in some trade or other, and did I expect my aunt or my mother to recognise the plumber? It sounds like snobbery; and why shouldn't it. It was."[3]

Flamboyant in his attire off the track, Gogarty carried that practice into competition as well. Brightly coloured waistcoats were exchanged for tailored singlets and scarlet shoes, fitted to scarlet pedal blocks. When representing Trinity he donned black, with a prominent gold crest, while his regalia for the Al Fresco Club consisted of a tasselled cap and singlets of assorted colours. The competition at his exalted level was cut-throat, on the track and off it. So much so that he deemed it wiser to cycle the hundred miles back to Dublin having won first prize of a gold watch up at Ballinafeigh, rather than risk retribution if travelling back down from the north by train. His account of that foray to the north is notable for its graphic description and sustained tension.

Life couldn't of course be just about cycle racing, not for one with such an inquisitive outlook. That innate curiosity had seen Gogarty make the acquaintance of a certain Arthur Griffith, recently returned from South Africa, where he had fought on the side of the Boers. They encountered in An Stad, a tobacconist's shop on the corner of Rutland Square. Susceptible as ever to hero worship, Gogarty immediately agreed to write for Griffith's newspaper, the *United Irishman*, first published in March 1899. Arthur Griffith became the founder of Sinn Fein, a movement, as distinct to a political party, intent upon winning self-determination for Ireland by dint of setting up an alternative Irish administration, effectively replacing Westminster and Dublin Castle. Gogarty proved an enthusiastic recruit to the cause.

The dramatic fall of Parnell, the "uncrowned king of Ireland", seemed to trigger a widespread dissatisfaction with Westminster and all associated with it among the Irish Catholic middle class. That category embraced those who did not depend upon the Castle and the establishment for their livelihood. The Americans had got rid of the British, Canadians ran their own country, while remaining part of the British Empire, and now the whites in Africa sought self-determination. However, the Irish reaction, instead of howling for independence yet again, knowing full well that Britain would never relinquish what it had come to regard as its 'back garden', took the form of a Gaelic revival. Douglas Hyde's Gaelic League had swept the country, with a dramatic resurgence of Irish culture comprising arts, theatre, music, literature and language. It had already attracted such as Horace Plunkett, pioneer of the co-operative movement to revive and advance Irish agriculture, George Russell, Lady Gregory, J. M. Synge and W. B. Yeats.

The return of the troops from the Boer War in June 1900 was enthusiastically acclaimed by the establishment, headed by the Viceroy, the Lord Mayor and that broad, monied band of vested interests that was collectively termed "castle society". *Irish Society* was their magazine. As such the editor was only to pleased to accept and publish an "Ode of Welcome" to the returning troops, victorious on behalf of the British Empire, on which the sun never set. Heresy in such circles to murmur that Her Britannic Majesty's finest had been repeatedly humiliated by "a crowd of Dutch farmers". The success of the issue, which verily galloped off the news stands and had sold out within an hour, had little to do with monarchist, martial or imperial sentiment, but everything to do with the "ode" on page 14. It had somehow escaped editorial vigilance that this apparent paean to the victorious troops was actually an acrostic. Composed in five four-line stanzas, the first letter of each line, read from top to bottom stated baldly: "The whores will be busy." It had Dublin laughing for months. Authorship was attributed to one Oliver St John Gogarty.

In the autumn of 1900 Oliver Gogarty was joined in Trinity College by his brother Henry, who was simultaneously entered at Kings Inns, Michaelmas Term. Their varsity careers proved starkly contrasting. Henry would graduate with a BA and was admitted to the inns as a qualified barrister in Hilary Term 1905. The marked difference in approach to academic endeavour would perhaps suggest that Henry, as a younger son, was under no illusions as to inherited wealth in store for him on attaining his majority in November 1903. The brothers differed also in their social and sporting proclivities. Whereas Oliver was happiest celebrating life as a man-about-town in his native Dublin, Henry heeded the call of the hunting horn, becoming a regular guest of Dick Burke MFH and his son of the same name in Grove, Fethard, headquarters of the Tipperary Foxhounds.

CHAPTER SIX

Gogarty's competitive cycling career ended abruptly in 1901. When three of his rivals attempted to ram him he let loose a string of oaths that was overheard by the judges. He was suspended for foul language. Deaf to all offers to appeal on his behalf for reinstatement, Oliver St John Gogarty turned his back on competitive cycling for good. Such a show of intransigence was widely construed as Gogarty cutting off his nose to spite his face. Nevertheless, he would contend in later years that his summary renunciation of cycle racing, with the temporary vacuum that it created in his life, alerted him to the cultural renaissance happening all round him. His immediate response was to enter for the Vice-Chancellor's prize for verse. The subject in 1901 was "The Centenary of R. L. Stevenson". Gogarty's ten-stanza tribute to the author of *Treasure Island*, who had died and been buried on Samoa in 1894, was awarded the gold medal and the £20 prize that went with it. Beginners' luck seemed to attend Oliver Gogarty in whatever sphere he tried his hand. And as to it being better to be born lucky than rich . . . hadn't he been born both?

Oliver Gogarty's cycling career might have been forsaken in a fit of pique, but distress calls could not go unanswered. So it was that on 22 June 1901 he found himself involuntarily in the Liffey yet again, rescuing a Mr Max Harris from drowning. For this and for his unsuccessful intervention at Balbriggan the previous year Gogarty was awarded another medal by the Royal Humane Society. Gogarty rarely spoke subsequently about his life-saving exploits. However, he did divulge to his daughter Brenda, who passed the story on to a younger generation, that the Max Harris episode had come close to proving fatal for both men. It seems that Gogarty realised, almost too late and to his own cost, that the man whose life he sought to save was equally determined on his own destruction. He was, in the Dublin phraseology of the time, "doing the Liffey". Only by stunning his quarry was Gogarty able to effect the rescue.

Freed from the demanding disciplines of competition cycling, Gogarty made some headway in his medical studies. Having commenced clinical work in the Richmond Hospital in 1899, he progressed through physiology and applied anatomy, attended surgery lectures under "Boss" Bennett and medicine under Professor James Magee Finny. In the same dilatory fashion he gained credits for pathology and midwifery lectures, as a prelude to undertaking operative surgery and practical pathology studies. It was all rather half-hearted and distractions were at every hand. Having given up cycling Gogarty could participate to the full in the hedonistic existence so enjoyed by his companions from the Royal, Vincent Cosgrave, Simon Broderick, John "Citizen" Elwood, along with Tom Kettle and James Joyce, "tacked on as a 'medical student's pal'".

"We were nearer to poetic drama than we shall ever be again. Intellectual life was astir. Joyce and I used to go to see how the actors were getting on with John Elwood, a medical student, who enjoyed the licence allowed to medical students by the tolerant goodwill of a people to whom Medicine with its traffic in Life and Death had something of the mysterious and magical about it. To be a medical student's pal by virtue of the glamour that surrounded a student of medicine was almost a profession in itself. Joyce was the best example of a medical student's pal Dublin produced, or rather the best example, extinct since the Middle Ages, of a Goliard, a wandering scholar."

The actors to whom Gogarty refers were involved in what was first called the Irish Literary Theatre, with which George Moore, Edward Martyn, Lady Gregory and W. B. Yeats were closely involved. Gogarty's first exposure to Yeats occurred when he and Joyce attended a play reading by Lady Gregory in the Nassau Hotel in 1901. Yeats was subsequently invited to one of Mrs Gogarty's "evenings", where Gogarty made his acquaintance for the first time. In October the same year *Diarmuid and*

Grania was staged, to a distinct lack of critical acclaim. Violet Martin was moved to comment: "If this is the lofty purity of the Irish drama I am indeed mystified." Discouraged, Moore and Martyn distanced themselves from the Irish Literary Theatre. The Fay brothers promptly filled the void, changing the company's name to the Irish National Dramatic Society, recruiting in the process twenty-year-old Padraig Colum, a clerk at the Kildare Street railway office.

Of Gogarty's cronies from his days in the Royal, Vincent Cosgrave, the atheist who rejoiced in medieval church music and aesthetic argument, was destined to outdo him as a 'chronic' medical student, while 'Citizen' Elwood – so called from his egalitarian greeting to others – disappeared briefly to Buenos Aires, returning with panache to qualify eventually through the Licentiate of the Apothecaries' Hall over a decade later. Tom Kettle retained his iconic status, a rare achievement in the Gogarty pantheon.

"Of all the wits and worthies I have met, and they were quite a few, one of the outstanding ones was Tom Kettle. He was young, buoyant, laughing, carefree, and gifted with an astounding power of breaking through an enemy's front with a wit like lightning."

Gogarty's growing reputation among his peers as raconteur, bon viveur, diseur and bawdy bard attracted the interest of such men-of-letters as George Moore, William Archer, Richard Best and George Russell. Dublin being a small and innately spiteful pool of gossip and wit, it was inevitable that Gogarty's antics should reach the ears of that remarkable collection of gifted eccentrics – the Trinity dons. In any case one of their number, Edward Dowden, Professor of English, had already taken the budding poet in hand, every ready to promote his protégé's interests. So it happened that those other towering intellects, who had brought Trinity to the height of its academic standing, John Pentland Mahaffy, the Hellenist, Robert Yelverton Tyrrell, Regius Professor of Greek and Henry Stewart Macran, Professor of Moral Philosophy began to show interest in one touted as the natural successor to Oscar Wilde. It was Gogarty's turn to feel uncomfortable. He described feeling "like a goldfish surrounded in the crystal sphere of knowledge, in which all I could do was go round and round."

Stephen Gwynn, a lifelong friend of Gogarty's, described the situation in Trinity at that time in his delightful, nostalgic, whimsical *Dublin Old and New*.

"The group of Senior Fellows when he [Dr Salmon] was Provost included Ingram, it included Abbott, both known to all specialists in their subjects; it included Palmer, perhaps the finest latinist of his day, and Louis Claude Purser, who might have disputed the title with him, if he had ever in his life claimed anything against anybody. But above all, from the general public's point of view, it included Mahaffy and Tyrrell, leaders of opposite camps, both of them wits in the sense that the word was applied to Burke and Dr. Johnson – and indeed wits in any sense whatever. There was also Traill, whom nobody could have called a wit and who got the better of both of them, being made Provost in succession to Salmon."

Which of them Salmon would have preferred is not certain, he had sharpened his tongue often on both. The most famous instance is his reply to Mahaffy, who had been saying that he was only whipped once when he was a boy, "and that was for telling the truth." "It cured you, Mahaffy," said Salmon. These elders of the College Board, so far as I could make out, tore each other like dragons in the primeval slime.

Mahaffy confirmed Stephen Gwynn's impression in his own trenchant style.

"Trinity College men may not be, as a rule, as polished as an Oxford or Cambridge man, but there is a rough strength about them that atones for other deficiencies. As Irishmen they are fluent talkers, and as Trinity College men they are independent talkers, free to utter their opinions, not guided by precedent, differing readily even from their teachers. A man is judged by his conversation, by his ability to take in new ideas, by a thousand things which cannot be enumerated, but which are taken as evidence against all artificial tests if they disagree with his critics' rough-and-ready ones. So, too, among the Fellows. They criticize one another openly and readily, but always with perfect honesty. Some years ago the Fellows criticized one another so severely that they almost put a stop to any of their body publishing books. Every unfortunate author was so sifted and pulled to pieces, that it required a man of very thick skin to brave their shafts. But the stranger who dines at the Fellows' table and enters the Common Room is, I believe, pleased with the vigour and liveliness of the conversation."[1]

Not since Oscar Wilde's days in Trinity had the dons "adopted" a student as they proceeded to do with Oliver St John Gogarty. George Moore, already an established novelist, who had moved back to his native land in protest against the Boer War, was outspoken in his praise of the ebullient undergraduate. "Gogarty is the Arch Mocker, the youngest of my friends, the author of all the jokes that enable us to live in Dublin, of the Limericks of the Golden Age, full in the face with a smile in his eyes, and always a witticism on his lips overflowing with quotations." Gogarty had a tall reputation to maintain among his middle-aged mentors, in what was an unfamiliar milieu for a Dublin Catholic youth. Mahaffy, the most arrant snob of this cerebral trio was reputed to have said of Gogarty's "medical students' pal" "James Joyce is a living argument that it was a mistake to establish a separate university for the aborigines of this island, for the corner-boys who spit into the Liffey." It was the same Mahaffy who had recommended that Oscar Wilde transfer to Oxford, where the demands on his intellect would not be as great. "Oscar, you are not clever enough for us here, you had better go to Oxford."

Mahaffy could have put it differently, echoing the anonymous wag who declared: "Every Scot who takes the highroad from Scotland to England raises the level of intelligence of both countries." But that would have been to raise the protégé to the level of his mentor; quite simply unthinkable.

Oscar had died in 1900, aged only forty-four, a broken man. His downfall, in Rebecca West's opinion, arose from a general failure to recognise that "the English male has from time immemorial been given to homosexuality. Sometimes this practice is due to a strong natural preference which lasts a lifetime, sometimes it is merely an artificial stratagem to overcome artificial barriers set up between the sexes, as used to be the case in colleges and schools. Care was taken by the British educational authorities to inflame the second conviction by overloading the curricula with Greek studies." She cited A. C. Benson: "If we give boys Greek books to read and hold up the Greek life as a model it is very difficult to slice off one portion which was a perfectly normal piece of life and to say it is abominable."

Observing that the double standards that made homosexuality a capital offence for so long under legislation enforced by those who had been involved in such practices at boarding school and cheerfully consigned their offspring to a similar fate, the doughty Rebecca cautioned her readers. "Do not try to work this out. It is simply an illustration of the tropism by which male minds feel an unreasonable desire to defend any unreasonable proposition." However, in lamenting the fate that befell the writer of *The Importance of Being Earnest*, "the only great comedy which had graced the English stage since Congreve's day," Rebecca West laid the blame squarely in one quarter.

It was an open secret that Wilde had been initiated into homosexual practices during a tour of the Greek Islands in the company of a celebrated professor, attached to a famous university, from which he was never, on this occasion or any other, called to separate himself. Indeed, he died as its Provost, in his eighties, rich in experience.

Oscar Wilde called his mentor at Trinity, "A really great talker in a certain way." Gogarty went further, "the finest talker in Europe." He was later to amend that opinion, describing the older man's efforts to encourage conversation in others as similar to the effect of a hawk on a couple of blackbirds. The author of *The Principles of the Art of Conversation* published in 1887 was equally renowned for his epigrams. "In Ireland the inevitable never happens and the unexpected constantly occurs." "An Irish atheist is one who wishes to God he could believe in God."

Walter Starkie, likewise a young disciple of Mahaffy's, was under no particular illusions concerning his mentor.

All his life Dr Mahaffy was renowned for his snobbery, but it would be very difficult to fit him into any of the categories of snobs enumerated by Thackeray, for he was too much of an Irishman and possessed too much wit and volatility of temperament. He wore his snobbery with such grace that it became an adornment to his personality and, besides, he would continually make fun of his own foibles. His snobbery sprang from his Anglo-Irish characteristics and it can be explained by a remark made by W. B. Yeats when he was asked whether Oscar Wilde was a snob: "No, I would not say that: England is a strange country to the Irish. To Wilde the aristocrats of England were like the nobles of Baghdad."

Just as Oscar Wilde had done, Gogarty rapturously embraced the concepts and ideals of the Greek model city state as Athens had been in its golden era, between 600BC and 400BC. That democracy was founded on beliefs and practices that seem strange indeed today. Women, it was held, were all potential nymphomaniacs from puberty. Accordingly, they were married off at the earliest opportunity to older men, becoming prisoners in their husbands' houses, used only for the procreation of future warriors. There were some exceptions, who became prostitutes, licensed by the state and installed in three distinct grades of brothel outside the city walls. Those in search of heterosexual pleasures found their needs satisfied in the brothel rather than the marital bed.

The warrior elite was encouraged to form close one-on-one friendships, based on the belief that one man would willingly die in battle to protect his particular chum. Much of their time was spent in the gymnasium, practising martial arts and perfecting their bodies. It was only when platonic relationships moved to another plane that the Greeks suffered military defeat, at the hands of Alexander the Great. Sodomy had softened these beauteous, but muscle-bound fighting men.

In the all-male society that was Greece in its golden age, older men were encouraged to become mentors of youth, just as Mahaffy and his colleagues in Trinity considered themselves two thousand years later. A youth who attracted the attention of an older man was bidden, with his father's consent, to a symposium, where much feasting and drinking took place. As the highlight of the symposium his mentor would present his chosen protégé to his friends and contemporaries as the star turn of the evening, the honoured guest. While anal penetration was not outlawed, neither was it considered essential or even necessary for carnal satisfaction.

The eventual liberation of women arose through the power and influence of one remarkable courtesan – Phriny. Whereas the vast majority of her colleagues sold their bodies for money, Phriny traded hers for power. She captivated the sculptor Praxitheles, who used her as his model for Aphrodite, the first effigy of the female nude that Greece had ever seen. The effects on Greek manhood of Phriny's manifest charms would seem to have triggered a sea change in Greek sexual mores, leading to the gradual elevation of married women to something approaching gender balance. Phriny didn't accomplish this conversion single-handedly. Aspasia employed the patronage of Pericles to equal effect in creating her highly influential establishment. Moreover, defeat at the hands of the Romans, who had always esteemed women, accelerated the change in Greek mores. This once invincible warrior race was at first appalled and then intrigued to learn about the female orgasm, an immediate legacy of defeat by the Romans. Mahaffy and his ilk would regard such developments as marking the end of the golden age of Greece.

Thus, when Gogarty declared his intention to "Hellenise Ireland", he cannot have been unaware of the underlying aspects of that cultural package. While such ideas may appear absurd in this day and age of promiscuity, they must be considered against the social mores of his age. At a time when a well brought up young woman's virtue was guarded to the point of paranoia, opportunities for dalliance were virtually non-existent. And the price of courtship was a proposal of marriage. Not infrequently the mildest romantic overtures could be misconstrued as proposition, resulting in lawsuit for "breach of promise", normally prosecuted by the scandalised parents of the jilted young lady. Unlike in England, Irish married women who had produced both the heir and the spare were not considered fair game. While divorce was available in Ireland at the time, it was seldom invoked.

CHAPTER SEVEN

Many years later Oliver Gogarty sought to explain the inexplicable by a variety of excuses, such as, "my head was in the clouds," or "I preferred to leave such matters to others." Perhaps he was afraid to raise the matter of his inheritance, as he would have been quite entitled to do on turning twenty-one. Instead he chose to sail blithely along, winning the Vice-Chancellor's Prize for Verse on a further two occasions, a Trinity record. It was at Joyce's instigation that he used his former association with the Royal University to enter for, and win, the Gold Medal for English Verse with "The Death of Byron". The medal was immediately pawned.

Undeterred by his senior colleague's lack of progress, James Joyce announced in the autumn of 1902 his intention to study medicine. Constantine Curran, his contemporary, was dismissive when Joyce mooted his idea while they walked on the North Bull Wall. Pragmatic as ever, Joyce retorted by saying that he could make sufficient money in a few years of practice to enable him to write in comfort for the remainder of his days. He did in fact enrol as a student in the College of Medicine in October 1902. In doing so Joyce was not merely imitating his drinking cronies, but actually following in his father's footsteps, for John Stanislaus Joyce had likewise embarked on his medical studies in Queen's College, Cork, in 1868. However, on coming into the first tranche of his inheritance when turning twenty-one in 1870, John Stanislaus promptly relinquished that phase of his existence. Instead he aspired to join an Irish company in the French Foreign Legion, only to be thwarted by his mother, who pursued him to London and brought him back to Cork.[1]

It was in August 1902 that James Joyce, known to his fellow-graduates simply as "The Hatter", bearded George Russell, in Garville Avenue, Rathgar, where he had been living for four years, married with two sons. "The Hatter" didn't pull his punches, declaring that "AE" lacked sufficient mental turmoil to succeed as a poet, while Yeats was sadly too old for Joyce to help. If this was an exercise in self-promotion, it achieved that aim. "AE" was sufficiently impressed to write to W. B. Yeats, then staying in Coole Park as Lady Gregory's guest. "This young fellow named Joyce . . . writes amazingly well in prose . . . engaged in writing a comedy which he expects will occupy him five years or thereabouts as he writes slowly . . . certainly more promising than Magee." "AE" subsequently claimed to have said of Joyce to Yeats, "The first spectre of the new generation has appeared . . . I have suffered from him and I would like you to suffer . . . of all the wild youths I have met he is the wildest." Indeed, "AE" continued to sing Joyce's praises for years to follow, moving Joseph Holloway to write, "Joyce at that time was the studied essence of conceit."[2]

Gogarty was to echo Joyce's arrogant dismissal of Yeats in a later recollection; one to which a degree of poetic licence must be accorded. As the interviewer observed, "I knew well before I finished, how far any man's statement was trustworthy or factual, but truth is not the whole of life, or facts the whole of truth, and these people [Irish literary figures] were, like myself, as honest as the day is long – and no more." On that understanding, this anecdote warrants repetition.

"We both lived on the north side of the city, and we were going up Rutland Square, I think it was a horse-drawn tram in those days. I happened to mention that thing the newspapers were full of – that it was Yeats's fortieth birthday and that Lady Gregory had collected from his friends forty pounds with which she bought a Kelmscott edition of Chaucer by William Morris. Everybody knew it was Yeats's birthday. But when I made an epiphany, so to speak, and told Joyce this, at the first tram stop he got out. Yeats was lodging in the Cavendish Hotel, in Rutland Square, and he solemnly walked in and knocked at Yeats's door. When Yeats opened the door of the sitting-room he said, 'What age are you, sir?' and Yeats said, 'I'm Forty.' – 'You are too old for me to help. I bid you good-bye.' And

Yeats was greatly impressed at the impertinence of the thing."[3]

True to his word, Joyce enrolled for classes in St Cecilia's, the Catholic medical school, in October, along with his friends John Francis Byrne and Seamus O'Kelly.[4] At the end of the same month he received his Arts degree. However, Joyce precipitately took himself off to Paris to continue his medical studies there, financed by a £5 subvention from Lady Gregory, who also provided him with an introduction to John Millington Synge.[5] His travels took him through London, where the inquisitive Yeats introduced him to Arthur Symons. The latter described the young Irishman as "a curious mixture of sinister genius and uncertain talent." Yeats wrote to Lady Gregory, saying that he found young Joyce "unexpectedly amiable . . . [he] did not knock at the gate with his old Ibsenite fury."

Inconsiderately, the French authorities refused to recognise Joyce's Dublin degree, thereby precluding him from the medical faculty. He turned to journalism and the companionable support of Fenian expatriates for survival. Homesick and worried about his ailing mother, Joyce failed to settle in Paris and returned home for Christmas via London, whence Yeats reported to Lady Gregory. "I have had Joyce all morning . . . He has now given up the idea of medicine and will take up literature. He said some rather absurd things and I rather scolded him but we got on very well."

By Richard Ellmann's account Joyce returned to Dublin to discover that he had forfeited the friendship of John Francis Byrne. The latter showed a postcard he had received from Joyce in Paris to Vincent Cosgrave, as evidence of their closeness. Cosgrave retaliated by producing a similar missive, but of a more earthy nature, disguised in "dog" Latin. Byrne felt betrayed.

"During Joyce's absence in Paris something had occurred which hurt me deeply. I cannot go into detail about this, but I felt so badly about it that I wanted to break with him. In long rambles about Dublin during the week after Easter, I talked the matter over with him exhaustively, but it seemed to me that his explanation explained nothing, and I would not agree to a continuation of our friendship. With this understanding, we parted finally on Friday night. On the following Sunday morning, the postman delivered to me this letter from James A. Joyce:

Dear Byrne,

Would you care to meet me tomorrow (Sunday) in Prince's St. at one o'clock? Perhaps you will not get this tomorrow morning as the post is upset.

J A J

7 S Peter's Terrace, Cabra

Saturday night

"In writing this letter to me Joyce proved that, in a way, he knew me better than I knew myself . . . That Sunday afternoon, evening, and night, we walked through all the southern suburbs of Dublin. And as we walked we talked; and gradually James Joyce won, in substantial part, his battle for a continued friendship . . . His explanation I did not accept – at that time; but he did succeed in convincing me of his sorrow . . . Notwithstanding our reconciliation, there was a modification in our relationship. This condition persisted for more than twelve months, but became gradually ameliorated, and by the time Nora Barnacle came into his life, James Joyce and I were again at one."[6]

Byrne's recollection of his break and reconciliation with Joyce was to prove of momentous significance for Joyce. It could even be said to have determined the writer's subsequent career. However, according to Ellmann, Joyce immediately filled the void by meeting Oliver Gogarty for the first time, in the Reading Room of the National Library; this being December 1902.

The young man was handsome, lithe though inclined to fat, prosperous, and merry. He introduced himself as Oliver Gogarty, and said he was taking a degree at Oxford. Gogarty was as addicted to obscenity and blasphemy as Cosgrave, and was also talented and the wittiest man in Ireland. He would one day be a famous surgeon and poet: that is, he would be famous as a surgeon to his readers and as a poet to his patients. The clerk from Oxford and the clerk from Paris, who was four years younger, began to consort together. Gogarty admired Joyce's poems, and proffered his own, which Joyce admired less.

Published in 1959, Richard Ellmann's *James Joyce* was so widely acclaimed that his inversion of Gogarty's standing as poet and surgeon became part of the Joycean myth, to the lasting detriment of Gogarty's posthumous reputation. Other commentators have pointed out that Ellmann's dismissive attitude to Gogarty is largely attributable to his unquestioning acceptance of Stanislaus Joyce's book, *My Brother's Keeper*. And Stanislaus had made it plain from the beginning that he disliked and distrusted Gogarty, particularly in terms of his influence on Stanislaus's adored elder brother, Jim.

Ellmann's snide synopsis of Gogarty's accomplishments in literature and medicine apart, the other inaccuracies in his account of Gogarty's "first encounter" with Joyce do not stand scrutiny. Aside from the convenience of substituting Gogarty for J. F. Byrne in Joyce's life story, there is no evidence whatsoever to advance December 1902 as the time of their first encounter. Indeed, it flies in the face of both Gogarty's memoirs, and Joyce's. It is equally absurd to suggest that Gogarty should have introduced himself as "taking a degree at Oxford." It is a matter of record that Gogarty did not enter Oxford until 1904. Finally, "fat, prosperous and merry" can only be warranted if used as counterpoints to the emaciated, impecunious and affectedly melancholic Joyce.

Fortunately for posterity, Gogarty's reputation was not to become Ellmann's exclusive preserve. W. R. Rodgers was to remember him as "the most generous man I ever knew," quoting Georgie Yeats, "the kindest heart in Dublin and the dirtiest tongue." Mrs Yeats elaborated on the apparent contradiction that Gogarty represented. "Don't you know that a man may do that [spread scandal] and still be the most loyal friend you ever had?"[7] Gogarty attributed Joyce's sense of being hard done by – "he had a dreadful sense of being wronged" – to the misery of his circumstances and home environment.

In his [John Stanislaus's] latter days he was a miserable provider. The landlords often used to pay the Joyces to clear out. They used to burn the banisters for kindling. The father was feckless. He didn't care anything about the family. He was drinking. He died of drink in the end.[8]

Joyce's eventual return to Paris in January 1903 to pursue a literary career drew the following comment from J. M. Synge in a letter to Lady

Gregory in March. "He seems rather badly off . . . unbrushed and rather indolent . . . French literature I understand is beneath him! [He is] being gradually won over by the charm of French life . . . coming back to Dublin in the summer to live there on journalism while he does serious work at his leisure." February had seen the wedding in Paris of Maud Gonne to John MacBride, she having converted to Catholicism. Like Arthur Griffith, John MacBride had fought on the side of the Boers against the British in Africa. They spent their honeymoon in Gibraltar and it was there that they plotted the assassination of Edward VII, or so Maud Gonne would later contend. Meanwhile, back in Dublin, May Joyce's health deteriorated inexorably. *T.C.D., A College Miscellany*, published the unsigned lampoon on Mahaffy, *The Death of Diogenes the Doctor's Dog* and 'The Big Wind' unroofed houses across the city.

CHAPTER EIGHT

James Joyce continued to eke out his hand-to-mouth existence in Paris until summoned home by telegram on Good Friday, 10 April 1903 – 'MOTHER DYING – COME HOME – FATHER.' In the meantime he had become sufficiently impressed by the works and personality of Arthur Rimbaud, to the point of imitating the artist's broad-brimmed hat and flowing cape. On the one hand this allowed the disciple to style himself the high priest of beauty, while on the other it gave him licence to bite whatever hand might feed him . . .

Initially diagnosed as suffering from cirrhosis of the liver, which was to appear on her death certificate, May Joyce was understood by her family to be in the throes of terminal cancer. By coincidence, she was under the care of Dr Bob Kenny, a neighbour of the Gogarty family in Rutland Square East. It had been his late brother, Dr Joseph E. Kenny, who had implored Parnell not to make his final, fatal journey to England twelve years earlier.[1] A devout Catholic, May Joyce had tried desperately to save her son Jim's soul before going to meet her Maker. For his part, James Joyce was prepared to acknowledge a God, but not to recognise any merit in conventional forms of worship. Gogarty's ostensible rejection of the Catholic Church and all it stood for sustained their friendship throughout that summer of 1903 as the younger man waited for his beloved mother to expire. The garden in Fairfield formed a sanctuary for the aspiring authors, away from the bustle and distraction of the city. Moreover, as the Joyce family were now living in Phibsborough, Fairfield was readily accessible to the troubled younger man. To add to James Joyce's woes, his alcoholic father had become increasingly irrational in the face of his wife's illness, exhorting her to recover or to die. John Stanislaus actually attempted euthanasia on at least one occasion, thwarted only by the intervention of sons Jim and Stannie.

For all Gogarty's overt iconoclasm and irreverence, his innate humanity overrode that pose, as he subsequently recalled in an interview with fellow-poet and broadcaster, W. R. "Bertie" Rodgers. "I hurt him tremendously by imploring him to go and pray beside his dying mother's bed. He refused to bend the knee and he never forgave me for being right . . . I was certainly right, for that woman was taught to believe that she had brought into the world a soul that could be damned forever, for all eternity. That was her beloved son, who would not bow down and pray with her. Then she passed into unconsciousness. And that's supposed to be an excuse. But, after all, there are times when you're not unconscious . . . He was very defiant about his religion. When he lost his faith it was a shock to him. And his answer was defiance."[2]

A widely publicised event, which occurred in Ireland on 2 July, can only have ignited Gogarty's lifelong fervour for fast cars and speed in all its forms. That was the 327-mile road race for the Gordon Bennett trophy around the roads of Kildare and Carlow. Victory went to the dashing red bearded Belgian, Camille Jenatzy, driving a 60-h.p. Mercedes. It will have struck a chord with Joyce as well, for *The Irish Times* of 7 April had carried his interview in Paris with Henri Fournier, one of three entrants chosen to represent France in the great international event. This turned out to be the only piece Joyce ever had published in his brief role as Paris correspondent for the Dublin newspaper. *The Irish Times* was delighted to herald the first international motor race to be staged in these islands. "The race is now one of the chief topics of conversation in Dublin. There is not a dissentient voice. Everybody is anxious to see the modern marvels perform their wonderful feats of speed under the control of the champion motorists of the world. It is not too much to say that Ireland is hungry for the race." The *Irish People*, a nationalist newspaper, waxed less lyrical. "The advent of these flittering crowds of vulgar, irreligious and soul-less foreigners among our people produces no lasting good, and is responsible for much permanent demoralisation.

"The real truth is that no English county council would undertake the responsibility of keeping a clear road for the potential suicidals and murderers, who are a risk to their own lives and imperil the lives of others in order to advantage the output of the English, French, German and American manufacturing firms . . . Happily, the landlords of past generations have seen to it that the country selected has been almost depopulated, so that if the people who remain are wise enough to keep a civil distance from the roads which they maintain, the casualties may be restricted to the visitors!"

Joyce was to get further mileage out of the 1903 Gordon Bennett when his article 'After the Race' was published in a December edition of the *Irish Homestead*. Curiously, the Gordon Bennett was staged in Ireland that year, through the offices of the Viceroy, specifically because the anti-motoring lobby in Westminster made such a lethal contest on public highways out of the question on the British mainland. Public antipathy aside, Britain's historic investment in canals and railways had been at the expense of its road system. There simply wasn't anywhere to stage such an event on the British mainland. Ironically, at the suggestion of Count Eliot Zborowski, one of the prime movers behind the race, the British cars were painted green as a tribute to the host country – thus was born "British racing green".

As a reaction to his father's behaviour and his own lack of money, James Joyce drank only sparingly during this period. However, following his mother's death on 13 August – a Thursday, the weekday on which *Ulysses* would be set – Joyce began drinking heavily. In this he was reputedly encouraged by Gogarty, who was quoted as saying that he was intent on "breaking his spirit" through alcohol. Nor did it help the relationship when Gogarty was quoted in the aftermath of May Joyce's death: "It's only Joyce, whose mother is beastly dead." The mother in question was just forty-four and had endured thirteen pregnancies.

The two met again after a few days' separation following May Joyce's death, when the following conversation is reputed to have taken place.

Gogarty: "Where have you been for two days? Were you ill?"

Joyce: "Yes."

Gogarty: "What were you suffering from?"

Joyce: "Inanition."

Gogarty, meanwhile, persisted with his medical studies, specifically in the fields of midwifery and gynaecology at the National Maternity Hospital, Holles Street, where his attendance was required at 32 deliveries, with personal responsibility for 12 of these. He took his BA at this time, as he was to recall in *Tumbling in the Hay*, in the chapter entitled: *Baccalaureus in Artibus*.

Oliver St John Gogarty was turning twenty-five when receiving his BA, four years after reaching his majority. His father, Dr Henry Gogarty, had died as long ago as 1891. While Mrs Gogarty may well have been a strong-willed and determined woman, it does seem strange that she should have been able to exclude her eldest son from any involvement in the family's finances. Nevertheless, such would seem to have been the case. In fairness to his mother, Oliver Gogarty's subsequent attitude to financial affairs might be held up as justification. On the other hand, by keeping him in the dark about the family finances for as long as she managed to do, Margaret Gogarty may have done more to promote her son's irresponsibility in such matters than to prevent it. Curiously, echoes of Mrs Gogarty's attitude were to resurface many years later in her granddaughter, Brenda, likewise left a widow at a comparatively early age. She maintained that no man was ready for financial responsibility before he reached forty!

CHAPTER NINE

Besides being conferred Bachelor of Arts in 1903, Gogarty also won his second consecutive Vice-Chancellor's prize for poetry. The subject was "The Death of Shelley". Thereupon Joyce pointed out that Gogarty was eligible to enter a similar competition in the Royal University for the Gold Medal, by virtue of being a former student. Gogarty described Joyce's suggestion as a "cryptogram", in that Joyce indicated that a successful outcome could achieve the redemption of Gogarty's rifle. It was a roundabout way of saying that Joyce had pawned the rifle that he had borrowed from Gogarty, without ever advancing a reason for so doing. It seems reasonable to assume that Gogarty knew full well Joyce's motive, and thus felt no need to enquire further. Moreover, the rifle in question had almost certainly belonged to his late father and was of no practical use to him.

Oliver Gogarty duly won the Gold Medal for his "Death of Byron". The medal was promptly pawned by Joyce, who sent the pawn ticket to Sir James Meredith, Chancellor of the Royal University. As Gogarty later noted, the rifle remained unredeemed. However, Gogarty's continuing success in university poetry competitions was to yield another, very different dividend. A chance encounter with R. W. Lee, a Fellow of Worcester College, in Macran's rooms led to Gogarty transferring to Oxford to try for the prestigious Newdigate Prize. This notion met with little or no resistance from either his mother or his aunt, who considered young Oliver's association with James Joyce potentially dangerous. Mrs Gogarty had even resorted to writing to Tom Kettle expressing concern that Joyce was luring her son into agnosticism.

Another who expressed his relief at Oliver Gogarty's disappearance from the Dublin scene was Joyce's younger brother, Stanislaus. Two years

Jim's junior, Stannie hero-worshipped his brother to the point of near-idolatry. He was openly fearful of Gogarty's influence on Jim. John Francis Byrne likewise came into Stannie's category of "dangerous to know". He referred to the latter as "Thomas Square-toes", describing Byrne as having "an impenetrable mask like a Cistercian bishop's face." Not that Stannie received much credit for his custodial role within the family. His drunken father described Stannie as "Jim's jackal," whose awareness of his brother's superior mind had given him an inferiority complex. Even Jim rejected his brother's role as protector, declaring that Stannie reminded him of Gogarty's description of W. K. Magee [otherwise John Eglinton] in that "he had to fart every time before he could think."

The Stannie-Gogarty duel inevitably threw up its share of epithets. In Stannie's view "Last-lap Gogarty", was shallow, dangerous and a most demoralising person, who fully deserved Stannie's nickname for him – *Punch*. Gogarty, who considered Stannie – six years his junior – a prig, referred to him as "Jim's Flemish brother." While Stannie recorded his feelings in his daily journals[1], venting his spite in lengthy passages, Gogarty resorted to his favourite *metier* – the limerick.

> *Poet Kinch has a brother called Thug*
> *His imitator, and jackal, and mug.*
> *His stride like a lord is*
> *His pretension absurd is*
> *In fact he's an awful thick-lug.*

In fairness to Stannie, who really did have his brother's best interests at heart, he did see and acknowledge some merit in Jim's relationship with *Punch*. "Gogarty has friendship for Jim . . . in the drab streets of Dublin, the stolid masks of secret and disappointed lives, he and Gogarty make a vital pair."

Months earlier, in the autumn of 1903, Arthur Griffith, whom Gogarty had come to admire in his propensity to create personal heroes, founded what was to become Sinn Fein, intended to achieve peaceful autonomy for the Irish nation. In Gogarty he had an ardent supporter on the political front, though not unreservedly so where the national cultural movement was concerned. Gogarty feared the "Celtic chloroform," that threatened to "freeze the Sapphic current of my soul." The "Celtic chloroform" became his term for the vogue in writing of ancient Irish heroes: "the epidemic of the disinterred." Joyce considered the Celtic contribution to European culture consisted solely of the "whine". Tom Kettle expressed a very, very, long-range aspiration when writing: "If Ireland is to become truly Irish, she must first become European." That metamorphosis remains some way from realisation.

Just before Christmas 1903 the Irish National Theatre Society produced Padraic Colum's play *Broken Soil* in Molesworth Hall. Reviewing it for the *United Irishman*, Gogarty praised it as "a national drama in a fuller sense, perhaps, than any yet presented," adding that it was blessedly free of "folk-smoke" and mysticism. As the only Catholic regularly writing plays for the INTS at that time, and an established crowd-puller, Padraic Colum was highly valued by the directors, so much so that W. B. Yeats had gone on record: "the loss of Colum would put [the directors] in an impossible position." It was the reality of Colum's themes that appealed to audiences to a greater degree than the mythology favoured by Yeats and Lady Gregory.

For all its trumpeted tradition of theatre, Dublin had sunk to a dismally low ebb towards the end of the nineteenth century. Of the three officially designated theatres in the capital, the Theatre Royal in Hawkins Street and the Gaiety in South King Street served up repeats of the mass-market shows that had succeeded in London, while only the Queen's Theatre in what is now Pearse Street aspired to anything more cerebral. And that did not exactly constitute a quantum leap, described by one theatrical historian as "a mythical land of blarney and blather, peopled by patriotic heroes of exclusively aristocratic descent, betrayed by villainous informers and mourned by impossibly innocent colleens." Against a background such as this it becomes easy to see why the plays of Synge in particular and the other Abbey playwrights in general engendered public outcry. They had never been confronted with what all too many realised was a mirror image.

CHAPTER TEN

On 25 January 1904, Oliver St John Gogarty entered Worcester College, Oxford, where the philosopher W. H. Hadlow became his tutor. The following month in a letter to Joyce he revealed, "I'm reading for a Litt. D which I don't intend to take out but it enables me to read with the lady students." As had been the case in Trinity, his reputation as a wit and a prankster soon spread, though in a more restrictive environment, where he perceived form as being more important than content. His natural exuberance and disregard for the niceties led to the alternative of drinking the sconce down in one or paying a fine. To one "weaned on pints" the challenge was irresistible. The sconce contained five and a half pints. . .

"I planted my elbows firmly on the table and raised the silver tankard to my mouth. I took a deep breath. I began to drink. The first two pints went down pleasantly enough. It would have been enjoyable if there had not been so much depending on the draught. You would never guess what effected me most. Not a feeling of repleteness. No. You would never guess.

"It was the awful cold that hurt me on both sides of the throat and went up into my ears . . . I held on, conscious still. If this goes on I will pass out; but on it had to go. I suppose it took two or three full minutes, and two minutes are enough to die in. Look at the second hand of your watch to realise how long two minutes can be. To me, whatever time it seemed ten minutes longer. At last I reached the bottom and I put my head back to drain the thing so that it would not drip when I held it upside down."

Although various stratagems to get Joyce over to share his Oxford experience failed to materialise, the two continued to correspond and confide in one another as the following letters, dated 10 March 1904, confirm.

"My dear Joyce, I am indeed sorry to have forsaken you in whom I am well pleased. Congratulations that our holy mother has judged you worthy of the stigmata. Pray fervently O my brother that you may gain increase of grace to remain worthy of them and bear the favour with becoming humility. As it would be absurd and pernicious for me to prescribe for a penis in a poke so to speak I enclose a letter for you to hand to my old friend Dr. Walsh one of the best. He will see you right for me and if you can be repaired repair you. How is the novel progressing. I have written a poem and am on a play.

"If I would venture an opinion – you have got a slight gleet from a recurrence of original sin. But you'll be all right. . . . Don't let any laziness prevent you from presenting this letter as it may become incurable if neglected or if you drink."

Enclosed, as promised, was a letter to Dr Michael Walsh.

"My dear Mick, A friend of mine has been seeking employment as a water-clock and as he has not met with much success would be glad if he could re-convert his urethra to periodic and voluntary functions. I take the liberty of asking you to advise him from this note as I cannot introduce him myself; being busy teaching the language to the natives here. Mr. Joyce is the name of the tissues surrounding the infected part if you will cure him and delight me. He may have waited too long and got gleet."

Joyce enthusiasts of a medical bent would subsequently seize upon Gogarty's use of the word 'gleet' as confirmation that Joyce was merely suffering from gonorrhoea, a relatively minor sexually transmitted disease. However, Kathleen Ferris, in her admirable expose – *James Joyce & the Burden of Disease* – was to argue that the relevant words in these letters are "recurrent" and "intermittent", both of which apply to the potential killer – syphilis.

Gogarty wrote to Joyce again on 3 May, captioning his letter: "The Bard Gogarty to the Wandering Aengus." "My dear Joyce: may'st gain Eurydice from the infernal ones on your descent today! I hope you will keep clear of the 'rout' that makes the hideous roar, in other words that the so long neglected ladies will not over come you afterwards. Wire immediately the result is heard, and raise, on the victory falling to you, 5£ and come here for a week . . . without faith we cannot be healed. Good luck old man: Give this 'to Elwood poxed'."

The enclosures included this parody of W. B. Yeats's "The Pity of Love". The 'Hunterian swelling' is a reference to the eighteenth century English physician, John Hunter, immortalised in medical history for having inoculated himself with gonorrhoea, only to die of syphilis, thereby dramatically disproving his contention that the two diseases were one and the same. Admittedly, the two can be contracted simultaneously, thus adding to the unfortunate Hunter's mistaken conviction. The "Hunterian swelling" represents a syphilitic chancre.

> *In the house where the whores are dwelling*
> *Unless it is wrapped in a glove*
> *A little Hunterian swelling*
> *Poxes the part that they love.*

Kathleen Ferris proceeded throughout her book to build a most convincing case to prove that Joyce had contracted syphilis, which was ultimately to prove fatal. She further contended that it was Gogarty's lighthearted mockery of Joyce's condition, which also causes impotence and balancing difficulties, that lay at the root of Joyce's subsequent antipathy, expressed in the character "Malachi Mulligan", Stephen's betrayer, not of causes but of personal misfortunes. Unlike George Moore, who used the name Oliver Gogarty in a novel for its double instance of three "delightful dactyls", Joyce did not adopt or in his case adapt "Oliver" to 'Malachi' simply for assonance. Malachi is "God's messenger" in the Old Testament, who foretells the return of Elijah.

Ever the extrovert, Oliver Gogarty continuously expanded his circle of friends and acquaintances. Dermot Freyer, destined to become a friend for life, introduced him to Francis Willoughby Tancred, who knew every word of Herrick. Samuel Chenevix Trench would later become an inmate of the Martello Tower in Sandycove. Compton Mackenzie and

Christopher Stone would cross Gogarty's path from time to time in the years ahead. But George Kennedy Allen Bell proved to be both friend and rival. The future Bishop of Chichester was awarded the coveted Newdigate Prize for his "Delphi", with Gogarty being awarded the *Proxime accessit*. And second best is always just that. He had failed to emulate Oscar Wilde, disappointing Dowden, Mahaffy, Macran and all those who had pinned their hopes on their TCD protégé. With becoming modesty Gogarty submitted both his poem and Bell's to Dowden's scrutiny, contending that Bell's was the deserving winner. Dowden did not disagree. Less palatable was George Moore's mischievous reaction, boosting Gogarty's ego by declaring: "By Jove, Gogarty, that Newdigate you showed me was splendid!" Only when Gogarty had swallowed the bait did Moore cut him down to size by adding that a "splendour" attached to Bell's poem; "You couldn't possibly have won it!"

A fleeting return in March to sit his medical examinations had yet again resulted in failure. Added to academic insult was financial injury. Joyce prevailed upon both Gogarty and John Francis Byrne for money to finance piano hire and singing lessons, initially from Benedetto Palmieri and then from the more affordable Vincent O'Brien, who had also coached John McCormack.

Stannie took up his pen and dipped it in vitriol once again in the aftermath of Gogarty's fleeting return. The entry in *The Dublin Diary of Stanislaus Joyce* for 3 April 1904 contained the following observation. "Gogarty is generally regarded as a dangerous companion. He is scarcely this until he is intimate, but he is certainly a most demoralising person intellectually . . . One thing can be said of Jim's friends – Colum, Byrne, Gogarty, Cousins and those, that they are good liars. The rest I doubt . . . Gogarty's hooked nose and pointed chin and rotund form remind me of Punch. He wears a Punch-built waistcoat."

A week later Stannie returned to the attack. "Gogarty is treacherous in his friendship towards Jim. While never losing an opportunity of 'keeping in touch' with celebrities to whom he is introduced, he affects to care nothing for them, or his own reputation, or anyone else's. He affects to be careless of all things and carries this out by acting generously towards Jim in regard to money . . . The truth is, Gogarty – and his mother believes him – hopes to win a literary reputation in Ireland. He is jealous of Jim and wishes to put himself before him by every means he can. The carelessness of reputation is the particular lie he has chosen to deceive himself with. Both Gogarty and his mother are mistaken, however, for Gogarty has nothing in him and precious little character, and is already becoming heavy, while Jim has more literary talent in him than anyone in Ireland except Yeats."

On 20 April Stannie recorded: "Jim is living in lodgings in Shelbourne Rd on money Gogarty lent him, and Byrne and Russell." Diaries can be damning. Joyce did not win the Feis, being awarded only third prize, a bronze medal, which he claimed to have thrown into the Liffey. Being bronze it had negligible value in the pawnbroker's. Encouraged to sing by his musically accomplished parents from his earliest days, Joyce by this time was an accomplished tenor, as Gogarty later recalled in *James Joyce As A Tenor*.

"I heard him sing one morning when I called at Shelbourne Road. His voice was clarion clear and though high pitched was not at all strident. His build may have been too slight for a successful tenor. I remember John McCormack, whose career began with a victory at the Feis, telling me that he could not reduce below 224 pounds without a change in the quality of his voice."

Gogarty duly conveyed his Oxford disappointment in a letter to Joyce. "This Danaan Druid, O Wandering Aengus, obtained but 2nd place in the Newdigate! Further cause for impecuniosity. My Alexandrines I think are not traditional – hence these tears – Damn tradition, and the impenetrability of Professors' souls but perhaps to damn tradition is to wreck Rome and England, and we must have the one as we must have lingerie – on ladies – and we require the other as the ladies themselves. However, good luck . . . O Aengus of the Birds. Sing sweetly so that the stones may move and build a causeway to Oxford."

In his "unpremeditated autobiography", written many years afterwards, Gogarty attempted to rationalise his Oxford triumphs and disasters. "On the whole, I'd rather have drunk the sconce than won the Newdigate. Oscar Wilde won the Newdigate and landed in Reading Gaol. G. K. A. Bell won the Newdigate and became Bishop of Chichester. And, latterly, it was won by a woman who, I am sure, could never have achieved the sconce. The way I was treated from that day on, you might think I had seen the Holy Grail."

Further reverses in his medical examinations saw Gogarty denied even the safe haven of 5 Rutland Square on his return, vanquished, from Oxford. In apologising for his inability to lend Joyce yet more money he wrote: "I am cut off from my domicile by the Mater. So keep room in that dust-bin of yours." Yet another examination failure meant that the maternal embargo on hearth and home was not lifted until June. That trusty old resource, the Vice-Chancellor's Prize for Verse, was not open to Gogarty in 1904, by virtue of his three consecutive victories, so he turned his attention to the equivalent for English prose. The success of his essay – "Mythology – theories as to its origin and development" – provided a timely boost not just to his battered ego but to his precarious finances as well. In its August issue *Dana* carried "To Stella", the first poem to appear under Gogarty's own name in a general publication.

CHAPTER ELEVEN

Could it have been entirely coincidental that the first reference to the famous tower episode in *It Isn't This Time of Year at All!* opens the thirteenth chapter of Gogarty's "unpremeditated autobiography"? "James Joyce said, 'Do you know that we can rent the Martello Tower at Sandycove. I'll pay the rent if you will furnish it'." The confusion thus begins, for in a letter to G. K. A. Bell in July 1904, Gogarty wrote a different account. "The latest: I have had a letter from the War office in answer to an enquiry of mine about renting the Martello Tower (towers which were erected at intervals of a few miles around the Irish coast to prevent landing troops during the Napoleonic scare) in which Joyce is to hold his estate. The rent will be only about 16£ a year and as he wont have to pay it the scheme is feasible. He must have a year in which to finish his novel. I'll send photos when we house the bard securely. The Tower stands on a high rock over the sea. 3 rooms & a space on top completely sheltered by a par[a]pet 6 feet high so that absolute privacy from all but seamen is assured."

Later that same month Gogarty wrote to G. K. A. Bell again. "The Bard is monetarily improving. He & I go next week into the Tower over the sea of which I spoke to you before. The Tower that 'looks towards Ben Adair' if not 'Namancos hold'. I shall write you to come over & stay until you meet Yeats & 'many more whose names on earth are dark'. Yeats is to stay and teach poetry to his pupils this autumn in Dublin. You must come across if only for a week. I shall furnish the tower with Chippendale sticks: no pictures. The Bard Joyce is to do the house keeping. He is to Watts-Dunton me also."

Towards the end of the same letter Gogarty indicated an ominous degree of indecision about his life. "Sometimes I actually contemplate returning to Oxford, but then I should have to remain at espiscopal [sic] Worcester where my supporters are gone down: Crawley, Whatley, & the few I cared about. No: I must stick here until I unburthen mine & burthen others' minds."

In his correspondence with G. K. A. Bell, Gogarty alluded to Joyce's increasingly insistent demands for money, while at the same time assuring Bell that he was not among Joyce's intended victims, though perhaps unconvincingly. Meanwhile Joyce had managed to get a few pieces published in the *Irish Homestead*, through the good offices of "AE" George Russell. The readers' reaction was such that editor H. F. Norman declined any further contributions. Constantine Curran, editor of *St. Stephen's*, then invited Joyce to submit anything he might have failed to get published elsewhere. Joyce responded with "The Holy Office". . .

Scandalised, Constantine Curran returned the "unholy thing", though not without a token payment; almost as a form of personal insurance against such malicious blasphemy. In a lengthy diatribe in rhyming couplets Joyce set himself apart from all other Irish writers, castigating them individually and collectively as hypocrites. Yeats was distracted by women, Gogarty was a snob, Colum a chameleon and Russell an ass. Gogarty reacted badly, determining to break with Joyce, as he wrote to G. K. A. Bell on 27 August. "I have broken with Joyce, his want of generosity became to me inexcusable. He lampooned AE, Yeats, Col[u]m & others to whom he was indebted in so many ways. A desert was revealed that I did not think existed in the seeming luxuriance of his soul, so."

As Gogarty had signed the lease on the Martello Tower on 29 July and the deed of conveyance most likely on his birthday, 17 August, his primary reason for taking the place had been nullified before it had even been realised. Stannie Joyce had reacted to news of the Martello Tower scheme with characteristic asperity in his diary entry for 31 July. "Gogarty acts on ill-informed, hastily conceived theories of conduct and thereby causes not a little inconvenience to his friends. As he was once a champion cyclist, I call him 'Last-lap Gogarty'. Need I say that his theories never work out against himself.'

Ironically, in the light of Joyce's condemnation of Yeats being distracted from the pursuit of his art by female charms, it was just such an infatuation that had given James Joyce the courage to turn upon his friends and benefactors. On 10 June, in Nassau Street, Joyce had first set eyes upon the woman who was to change his life forever – tall, auburn-haired, twenty-year-old Nora Barnacle.

CHAPTER TWELVE

In the film *Nora*, Gogarty and his chronic medical student friend Vincent Cosgrave are shown as meeting Joyce and Nora out walking. The encounter moves Gogarty to remark to Cosgrave: "Well, at least there's one thing, the bard is no snob." Even if that jibe were a piece of poetic licence, Gogarty would have known that Nora came from Galway and was then working as a chambermaid in Finn's Hotel in Leinster Street. In the light of subsequent developments it is safe to assume that Gogarty mentioned the Galway girl with the unusual surname to his mother, however obliquely. Mrs Gogarty recalled a journeyman baker of the same name who had worked for her father, John Oliver, in Galway – Thomas Barnacle. Annie, his dressmaker wife and mother of seven, had eventually thrown her inebriate husband out of the family home in Bowling Green. The kindly illiterate with a weakness for drink subsequently worked for many years in Byrne's Bakery in Oughterard. Nora was later to lament that it had been her fate to emulate her mother in marrying a drinker. While Gogarty was to get the credit or the blame for Joyce's partiality for alcohol, it seems fairer to say that alcoholism is generally accepted as being hereditary and Joyce's father was no teetotaller.

By his own admission Joyce was infatuated with the chambermaid from Galway, who seemed able to release him from his deep-seated Catholic inhibitions and associated complexes and encourage him to behave naturally. At least on occasion Nora contrived to defy the old adage: you can take the man from the bog, but not the bog from the man. She contrived, by a mixture of feistiness, candour and feminine wiles, to liberate Joyce from his preoccupation with his inner self and his mission to become a famous author. Joyce's obsession with Nora explains both Stannie's catty comment about Gogarty "causing not a little inconvenience to his friends" and Joyce's reluctance to move out of Dublin to the Martello Tower in faraway Sandycove.

The intervention of a woman in Joyce's life so surprised and disconcerted his friends that one of them, Vincent Cosgrave, took it upon himself to vie for Nora's affections. His advances were firmly repulsed by the strong-willed Galway girl, who turned a deaf ear to Cosgrave's warnings that Joyce was mentally unstable and would inevitably prove unfaithful. When Nora informed Jim of his friend's treachery the disclosure only strengthened Joyce's love for her. If Nora would consent to join him, Joyce determined to exile himself from Ireland, the better to pursue his literary career. Cosgrave's rejection by Nora seemed to accelerate the decline of his fortunes.

Despite Joyce's defection, Gogarty went ahead with his plans to occupy the Martello Tower, inviting James Starkey and Samuel Chenevix Trench to share his bizarre abode in Sandycove. He provided a detailed description when writing to G. K. A. Bell.

"In this tower there are four rooms. One large one above, and three below. Two of these are only pantries one containing a well; the other is copper-sheeted & was a magazine when the place was used as a fort. The upper chamber in which I now write, & where the apostles assemble on occasion, is reached by a ladder stairway & is about 20 feet off the ground. The walls are 9 feet thick & the door massive. But the best place of all is the roof. It is circular – the rooms are fairly square, (on two sides and two sides curved), and has a parapet all round. The parapet is about 6 feet high but there is a ledge a yard wide which, when one stands on it, enables one to see comfortably over the wall leaning arms on it. One may take sun baths unbeholden all day – if it shines. The view is splendid. Howth, to the north the mountainous arm of the Bay, changing with every cloud & affording wonderful successions of colour. Pink on a hot and sunny day. Purple or cerulean on clouded days. And, on days when there is an intermittent sunshine the hill gleams yellow as if clothed with fields of corn. (All right! Starkey and I have patented this! 'The barren steeps in faery fields of corn'). To the South, that is behind one looking to Howth – Professor Dowden is on Howth at present – Killiney stands; a tricipetal hill, the middle head of which is cursed by an obelisk – a beauty blasting sight."

The above is just one extract from a lengthy and typically discursive letter that mirrors Gogarty's feelings of relief at having severed relations with Joyce. The sense of release is palpable from the point at which the writer alludes to it. Indeed, the lyrical episode of the lobster accentuates that impression. "I bought a lobster to-day alive. And when I put him in a little pool his marvellous colours reappeared freshly so that I resolved to restore him to the 'great sweet mother' & I took the twine off his claws and sent him seaward. I suppose they'll catch him again if he has not taken his experience to his ganglion. I am without him to supper now but perhaps it is better to have him feed whatever little of the Idea is in me with the beauty of his colouring than to supply my more transient need with the muscles inside his skeleton. Surely I'm not a Christian? No; the Galilean incidents around the lake: filling nets with fish & actually increasing other takes proves that I have not imitated. My lobster is now wandering in the weird submarine moonlight which they say is visible night & day by the animalculae at the sea-bottom and stretching his stiffened joints & (if he could) wondering had he been to Hades & gained a rebirth."

The whimsy in this epistle carries right through to its conclusion. "Take as long as you like to answer this. I know you well enough now not to impose the return of an essay of yours for a rigmarole of mine. Jot down anything you care to do from time to time & send it to me fortnightly & monthly. I can always write, the difficulty is to stop without doing harm. My conversation, I know distracts when it doesn't bore but it can do both. So I fear lest I sin likewise on paper."

CHAPTER THIRTEEN

Gogarty had met his house guest Richard Samuel Chenevix Trench through the St Patrick's Club at Oxford, of which both were members. He was a grandson of Richard Chenevix Trench, Archbishop of Dublin in the latter part of the nineteenth century, and the son of a distinguished soldier, Major-General Trench. The latter had taken his own life in 1894. Despite his inherently Anglo-Irish background, Chenevix Trench had become an ardent convert to the Gaelic League, to which end he had taken the name Dermot by deed poll in 1903, re-styling himself simply Dermot Trench. During his summer vacation from Oxford, Trench had gone canoeing around the waterways of Ireland, thereby completing his education about Ireland and the Irish, as he believed. When Gogarty first mooted having Trench to stay as his guest in the tower, he had been warned that the Balliol man was prone to bouts of mental instability and depression.

Fellow house guest James Starkey – destined to make his literary reputation as Seumas O'Sullivan – was a pharmacist and son of William Starkey, physician and apothecary. Already making a name for himself as a poet, essayist and author, Starkey even turned his hand to acting as an enthusiastic supporter of the Irish artistic renaissance. Possessed of a typically Dublin sense of humour, he was both a match and a foil for Gogarty. Of his many wisecracks recalled by Austin Clarke in his memoir, *A Penny in the Clouds*, the one concerning the sulky carpenter warrants repetition. Starkey remonstrated with a carpenter over shoddy work, whereupon the artisan muttered that Christ himself had been a carpenter. Quick as a flash came the retort: "What about the scab that made the Cross?"

Gogarty's invitation to Starkey to join him in the tower was couched
in verse, in a short piece called "To Stark to leave Rathmines"[1].

To leave Rathmines and come down to the sea
I would persuade thee, Starkey, with these lines
So that men won't forget me who got thee
To leave Rathmines.
Here green trees drink the sea-blue air, and we
May look on rain or mountain when it shines
And it will shine for me if thou'll agree
To leave Rathmines.

Starkey was equally adept at turning a line with specific intent, notably
when Yeats, who accused Starkey of plagiarism, was asked his opinion
of Starkey. "Why should a wise dog praise his fleas?" Understandably
incensed, Starkey penned this riposte:

I too, with Ireland, loved you long ago
Because you sang, as none but you could sing.
The cause we held the dearest; now I know
How vain your love was, and how mean a thing.
And not to you whose heart went anywhere
Her sorrow's holy heritage belongs:
You could have made of any other air
The little careful mouthfuls of your songs.

James Starkey's sojourns in Sandycove would appear to have been
intermittent, for no account exists of his presence there during those
fateful days in September when James Joyce belatedly clambered up the
rope ladder and stepped through the stout oak door into the granite
fastness of the Martello Tower. Received wisdom would hold that Joyce
inveigled himself into the tower to obtain material for a projected book.
However, it is equally true that he had run out of alternative refuges.
Failure to pay his rent had seen him put out of 60 Shelbourne Road. His
relationship with Nora Barnacle effectively precluded his return to the
family home, 7 St Peter's Terrace, Phibsborough, (reclassified 5 St Peter's
Road in 1905). His father would have been scandalised by the notion of

his eldest son and heir consorting with a penniless skivvy of low birth.

As he had in June – on the night of 15-16 – Joyce initially stayed with James and Gretta Cousins in Sandymount and then with a medical student, James O'Callaghan, before moving in with his uncle, William Murray in 103 North Strand Street, Fairview. However, Joyce's nocturnal comings and goings upset his host to such an extent that he barred his dissolute nephew from the house. In fact Joyce's moving into the tower and thus under Gogarty's roof was effectively making a virtue out of a necessity. As usual, Stannie glossed the reconciliation to Gogarty's discredit in his diary entry, 14 September 1904. "At present he [Jim] is staying on sufferance with Gogarty in the Tower at Sandycove. Gogarty wants to put Jim out, but he is afraid that if Jim made a name someday it would be remembered against him (Gogarty) that though he pretended to be a bohemian friend of Jim's, he put him out. Besides, Gogarty does not wish to forfeit the chance of shining with a reflected light. Jim is scarcely any expense to Gogarty. He costs him, perhaps, a few shillings in the week and a roof, and Gogarty has money. Jim is determined that if Gogarty puts him out it will be done publicly. Cousins and Mrs. Cousins, especially, invited Jim to stay for a fortnight, but Jim found their vegetarian household and sentimental Mrs. Cousins intolerable, and more than this he did not like their manner to him. They made no effort to induce him to stay longer."

Stannie went on to examine his own paranoia, induced by living in his brother's shadow. "Cosgrave and Byrne and Gogarty and in fact everyone who knows us is anxious to accuse me of aping Jim . . . Gogarty told Jim once that I was an awful thug, that I was grossly affected in manner, a 'washed-out imitation of Jim', and added that there was only one freak in the family. I admitted that my manner was affected, was a manner in so far as it was affected. Jim agreed and went on to detail how I did not imitate him. As I saw Jim had made up his mind and would believe me only – to use St. Augustine's phrase – 'when I confessed unto him', I said 'Hm.' Cosgrave too thinks I imitate Jim, but these people bore me and I really do not care a rambling damn for their opinions good or bad. I really despise them all – Colum, Starkey, Gogarty, Byrne, even Cosgrave.

I despise them because I cannot do otherwise."

Having thus dismissed his critics and mockers, Stannie turned his chilling gaze upon his idolised brother, Jim. "I hate to see Jim limp and pale, with shadows under his watery eyes, loose wet lips, and dank hair. I hate to see him sitting on the edge of a table grinning at his own state. It gets on my nerves to be near him then. Or to see him sucking in his cheeks and his lips, and swallowing spittle in his mouth, and talking in an exhausted husky voice, as if to show how well he can act when drunk, talking about philosophy or poetry not because he likes them at the time but because he remembers that he has a certain character to maintain, that he has to show that he is clever even when drunk, and because he likes to hear himself talking. He likes the novelty of his role as dissipated genius. I hate to hear him making speeches, or to be subjected to his obviously and distressingly assumed courteous manner. He is more intolerable in the street, running after every chit with a petticoat on it and making foolish jokes to them in a high weak voice, although he cannot possibly have any desire, his organ of generation being too weak for him to do anything with it but make water. They – the little bitches – run screaming away in pairs and then come back to see if he will chase them again. Jim courts this wasting and fooling although he knows it to be an insinuating danger. He tried it first as an experiment, then he got drunk in company for the want of something more interesting to do. He welcomes drunkenness at times, hoping to find in it some kind of conscious oblivion, and finding I don't know what."[2]

CHAPTER FOURTEEN

In the light of the enormous and enduring literary significance of Joyce's brief sojourn in the tower, aficionados of *Ulysses* must be forever indebted to one William Bulfin[1], who was gathering material for his *Rambles in Eirinn* at this very time. He and a companion were cycling out of Dublin in the Dalkey direction on a lovely, sunny September Sunday morning, which has to have been 11 September, when his fellow-cyclist mentioned "two men living in a tower down somewhere to the left who were creating a sensation in the neighbourhood. They had . . . assumed a hostile attitude towards the conventions of denationalisation, and were, thereby, outraging the feelings of the *seoinini*." Bulfin needed no second bidding.

"There was no necessity to repeat the suggestion, so we turned off to the left at the next crossroads, and were soon climbing a steep ladder which led to the door of the tower. We entered, and found some men of Ireland in possession, with whom we tarried until far on in the morning. One of them had lately returned from a canoeing tour of hundreds of miles through the lakes, rivers, and canals of Ireland, another was reading for a Trinity College degree, and assiduously wooing the muses, and another was a singer of songs which spring from the deepest currents of life. The returned marine of the canoe was an Oxford student, whose button-hole was adorned by the badge of the Gaelic League – a most strenuous Nationalist he was, with a patriotism, stronger than circumstances, which moved him to pour forth fluent Irish upon every Gael he encountered, in accents blent from the characteristic speech of his alma mater and the rolling blas of Connacht. The poet was a wayward kind of a genius, who talked with a captivating manner, with a keen, grim humour, which cut and pierced through a topic in bright, strong flashes worthy of the rapier of Swift. The other poet listened in silence, and when we went on the roof he disposed himself restfully to drink in the glory of the morning."

Joyce, the silent member of these three "men of Ireland", would immortalise the Gaelgoir Trench as Haines, the Swiftian one as Buck Mulligan and the silent member as Stephen Dedalus in *Ulysses*. Gogarty would provide his own account in his "unpremeditated autobiography" and elsewhere. Countless others would subsequently hypothesise to their hearts' content about what did or did not occur in the Martello Tower in September 1904. Numerous other visitors invited to the tower at this time were themselves writers, among them George Russell, Dermot Freyer and even Arthur Griffith. However, it is to the casual caller William Bulfin, travelling around Ireland by bicycle that we owe this delightful vignette of life in the tower through the eyes of an independent, fascinated observer.

Bulfin had pedalled his way far southwards before the bizarre episode in the tower on the night of 14 September provided James Joyce with the opportunity he now sought to make his escape, firstly from Gogarty and secondly from Ireland. Joyce's account is there for all to read in the opening chapter of *Ulysses*. Gogarty dealt with it later in his "unpremeditated autobiography", *It Isn't This Time of Year at All!*

In his biography of Joyce Richard Ellmann duly gave his version, pointing out beforehand that, "Joyce and Gogarty did not get on without tension."[2] In further justification for what was to follow, Ellmann continued: "Gogarty evidently feared that Joyce might turn into a permanent and rather hostile dependent. Joyce was too concerned with Nora to treat Gogarty with any ceremony." Those two observations might seem contradictory, but contradiction had already become Joyce's stock in trade. And if Ellmann had begun to flounder at this point in his own Anna Livia Plurabelle, Gogarty clearly considered his lifesaving days behind him. When approached by Ellmann in 1954 for an interview for his James Joyce biography, Gogarty declined. Undaunted, Ellmann gave his account.

"In cold prose Joyce regarded himself as put out of the tower. What happened was that during the night of September 14 Trench began to scream in his sleep. He was convinced that a black panther was about to spring. Half waking, he snatched his revolver and shot at the fireplace beside which Joyce was sleeping. After having despatched his prey, he turned back to sleep. While Joyce trembled, Gogarty seized the gun. Then Trench, again ridden by nightmare, screamed and reached again for his revolver. Gogarty called out, 'Leave him to me', and shot not the panther but some pans hanging above Joyce's bed, which tumbled down on the recumbent poet. The terrified Joyce considered this fusillade his dismissal; without a word he dressed and left, having – at that hour – to walk all the way to Dublin. When the National Library opened he told Magee, who was on the staff there, what had happened to him. The same day, back in the reluctant bosom of the Murrays', he sent a note to James Starkey asking him to pack his trunk at the tower so it could be picked up on the day following."

The note from Joyce to Starkey was quite specific. "My trunk will be called for to-morrow (Saturday) between 9 and 12. Kindly put into it a pair of black boots, a pair of brown boots, a blue peaked cap, a black cloth cap, a black felt hat, a raincoat and the Ms of my verses which are in a roll on the shelf to your right as you enter. Also see that your host has not abstracted the twelfth chapter of my novel from my trunk. May I ask you to see that any letters coming to the Tower for me are redirected to my address at once?" Having exhausted his welcome everywhere else, Joyce reluctantly sought refuge in the family home, ever fearful that some stray remark would betray his relationship with Nora to his erratic and irascible father. Meanwhile he secured a firm commitment from Nora to accompany him into the reckless uncertainty of exile. Borrowing all he could from any still prepared to "lend" to him, James Joyce left Ireland on 8 October 1904, with Nora surreptitiously at his side. Only Joyce's death would separate this unlikely couple.

From then onwards Joyce would insist that he could only write about his native city to best effect by distancing himself from his subject matter, while at the same time ensuring that he was kept informed in detail of all that occurred there. However, in both *Ulysses* and *Finnegans Wake*, the author goes to considerable lengths to suggest that his motives may have been entirely different. Furthermore, by condemning himself to living this lie and living with the consequences of this lie, both "Germ's Choice" and "Shame's Voice" became appropriate pseudonyms.

The likelihood is that Joyce fled his native country, ashamed of having contracted syphilis, which had proved incurable, as Gogarty had hinted might turn out to be the case. The disease has long been associated with the shame and guilt of sexual transgression – God's revenge. When the disease first erupted in Europe, victims were segregated and shunned, like lepers, like AIDS sufferers. The "fearful Jesuit" could not live with the notion that Gogarty, Cosgrave and others were likening Joyce to "Sinbad the Sailor" round the pubs of Dublin. Gogarty, particularly, resorted to mirth in the face of misfortune.

Whereas Constantine Curran readily accepted Gogarty's penchant for making fun of his friends' misfortunes as a means to amuse, others were less favourable, notably Padraic Colum, albeit writing in *Our Friend James Joyce*. "He had a defect that prevented his being a companionable man – the gravest of defects, perhaps: he had no reserve in speaking about people, even those whom he had cause to admire, even those who were close to him. If they had some pitiful disability or shortcoming, he brought it right out. It was an incontinence of speech with Gogarty that was in itself a defect. One might think it was for the sake of making a witty point that he maligned others, and sometimes it was that. But, exposed to it for a while, one began to see that the trait was basic: Oliver Gogarty could not help but see some oddness, infirmity, or delinquency in a person talked about. The result was that people gave him license and kept a distance from him."

That, as it transpired, was very much the Gogarty that Joyce was to portray in his caricature, "Buck Mulligan", and one that Joyce aficionados were destined to accept without question. Happily, Frank O'Connor – in the unlikely medium of *Leinster, Munster and Connaught* – redressed the balance.

"When, bogged in debt, Joyce left Dublin for ever he wrote and had printed a savage doggerel against those who had been foolish enough to lend him money, and circulated it to them by way of repayment – not the gesture of a young man mad with conceit, though Joyce had plenty, but of one incapable of accepting the burden of gratitude, who has no choice but to declare himself emotionally bankrupt.

"By cutting himself off from Ireland he became the prisoner of his memories. The 'paralysis' which he defined as the quality of Dublin which he wished to capture in *Dubliners*, his first book of stories, is the same which we find in *Portrait of the Artist, Ulysses* and *Finnegans Wake*, and between these astonishing books the development is technical, not intellectual. Being entirely passive, the material was responsive to endless technical development, so that Joyce could treat it rather as a professor than as an artist. In him the detachment of the artist has become prodigious and abnormal. An academic friend, defending *Ulysses* against my criticism, said mildly that 'it was a professor's idea of how a novel should be written'. There is considerable truth in this. Joyce was the first of the PhD writers, of whom Eliot is a later example . . . In his modest way Joyce proclaimed that he expected any reader to devote a lifetime to the study of his work. What he really meant was that he wrote entirely for PhDs who had nothing better to do with his time. There will, I fancy, be a terrific reaction against PhD literature from which the work of its masters will never recover. When pedantry becomes unfashionable it remains unfashionable."[3]

CHAPTER FIFTEEN

In an undated letter to George Bell, Gogarty refers obliquely to Joyce's departure from the tower.

"Trench & I are here still. Trench stays until 15th when he goes up again to Balliol – his last term. I shall linger here until I finish the work I am at now. I intend this as a refuge from the mortalia – an asylum I fear many call it from my methods in the locality. Trench will tell you particulars. The sea scape is gorgeous. 'AE' did an oil from the top last Sunday here. A friend of Trench Freyer a Cantab. called here & photographed us & it. So I can send you one of those photos when he sends them on. Freyer is a Yeatsian. He took Yeats around Cambridge when Yeats appeared there to lecture . . . Trench is delightful: erratic and neurotic but this latter is getting better with the sea air."

Curiously, Gogarty makes no reference to Joyce's leaving Ireland in his surviving letters to Bell. However, his October missive to Dermot Freyer duly put a characteristic interpretation on Joyce's disappearance. "The Bard Joyce has fled to Pola, on the Adriatic. A slavey shared his flight. Considering the poet's preaching and propensity the town he has chosen for the scene of his future living is not inappropriately named."

As Joyce noted in a letter to Stannie, he and Nora had been spotted together on their emigrant ship by John Joyce's friend, Tom Devin, who was quick to inform John Stanislaus Joyce that Jim had not been totally forthcoming. In a town where everybody knew everyone else's business – often rather better than his own – this news inevitably reached Gogarty on his daily missions into Dublin. Even had it not, he was going to be embroiled, because the distraught Annie Barnacle had written to Mrs Gogarty, whom she knew from the latter's early years in Galway, appealing for information on Nora's whereabouts. By this time anything to do with James Joyce was anathema to Mrs Gogarty, who detested her son's involvement with that profane young man. Nor did it improve matters that Mrs Gogarty had begun to suffer from both bronchitis and emphysema, which were to become chronic.

Gogarty wrote twice to his friend George Bell in October, referring to the departure of Dermot Trench in both instances. "Trench has gone back to Oxford. I did not see him for the last three days as, owing to an exam, I had to leave the lonely Tower and come in here to read for the satisfaction of some Doctors. I hope Trench is not annoyed. He could not sympathize with my Boe[o]tian existence in the Tower. The fact that all the nine came down into Boe[o]tia – the Theban villager Apollo's guest friend – could not satisfy him . . . Starkey, the singer of the twilight, (Celtic twilight, too,) will reside with me during the Winter as the carpenter is now arranging my abode. Trench dined us (at our insistence) on his birthnight. He could not appreciate the result. Starkey says I swam 'sub lunia' but she indeed had hidden her head . . . In response to Trench's constant assurances that everyone should learn their country's language – he himself speaks Gaelic well – I have procured a book of *modern Greek* and shall sail to 'where our east looks always to thy west, Our mornings to thine evenings, Greece to thee.' . . . I shall sail for Athens in a fruit and wine vessel next April & have three or four weeks in Athens for – all told – less than 30£. The Celtic chloroform will otherwise repress my 'noble rage' and freeze the phallic current of my soul."

Later that month Gogarty wrote again to Bell concerning Trench's departure. "I went out to Sandycove last night to find that Trench had gone, taking my sacred, chryselephantine shaving-brush with him. I readdressed any letters that were there to him, with the inscription 'not known at the town'. He has bearded me in my den or attempted to do so. I would not care so much if he had not, by leaving his brush as a substitute, suggested that they were coequal. The only personal extravagance and luxury that I indulge in are summed up in that frond-like brush. I have wired to Balliol about it. These things make life important!

"I have now to go out to Sandycove & see what he has done with the key

Oliver St John Gogarty by Orpen, c.1911

Oliver St John Gogarty, c. 1904

Mary Florence 'Mayflo' Gogarty

Martha 'Neenie' Gogarty with her children (L to-R) Dermot, Brenda and 'Noll'

Oliver St John Gogarty – cycling champion

Henry Hallam 'Harry' Gogarty

Renvyle House, Connemara

Richard 'Ricardo' Gogarty, Argentina, 1935

of the Tower. He went to England without informing me of his intention to go. I am rather anxious, because if he has left the key in the grass beside the place it is possible the fishermen or tramps will have entered it."

A year of mixed fortunes carried through in similar vein into 1905. Oliver St John Gogarty was awarded the Vice-Chancellor's Prize for English Verse for a third time when his *Cervantes: Tercentenary of Don Quixote* was adjudged the winner after a re-contest. That situation arose over confusion as to the eligibility of Gogarty's entry, which was initially thought to have missed the 1 January deadline. Gogarty described the confusion in a letter to G. K. A. Bell in January 1905.

"I was writing verse on Cervantes – 112 lines in 8 days – & it was awful work. I shall send you the thing when I get it back from the Judges & have it printed. It was for the Vice-Chancellor's verse & my last shot, as I have got it 3 times. When the results first appeared my nom de plume did not appear. After enquiry I found that the Senior Lecturer had not received it in time. So he said. Luckily, with great trouble, I could prove that it was sent in on the 1st as required. They held a second exam & I got 1st - £20. I should have only got about £10 as they cut one for going up so often, if they can. They cut the man who got it once before £5 and gave him £15. Then when they had to hold another exam, he became second & I must get £20 to make a first. So Mahaffy's mistake means £10 for me."

Unfortunately, similar success did not attend his medical examinations. While he managed to get through physiology, anatomy proved his downfall. In that field Gogarty could only console himself with the reflection that his practical courses in the Richmond Hospital were progressing favourably under the auspices of Sir Thornley Stoker, Professor Joseph "Joc" O'Carroll and Sir Thomas Myles. Adding insult to injury was Mrs Gogarty's insistence that her eldest son make a week-long retreat in a Cistercian monastery, the Abbey of St Marcellin.

If Mrs Gogarty thought that such an incarceration would reinforce her son's wavering faith, his observations on the experience to his friend Bell would have swiftly disabused her of that pious notion.

CHAPTER SIXTEEN

In the same month that Gogarty was expressing his views on the futility of monastic life to Bell, George Moore, an established and always controversial author, published *The Lake*. The principal character in this novel was an Irish country priest experiencing 'trouble with his vocation', having driven the pretty young teacher Rose Leicester out of his parish. Moore gave him the name Father Oliver Gogarty. Wise to the older man's flair for publicity and determined that his mother should not see the book and issue libel proceedings, Gogarty sent the offending book to Bell.

'I hope to go to some part of Germany for a few weeks at Xmas. You are lucky in going to Paris. I wish I could meet you there. I can easily get an introduction to Renan from Moore who owes me gratitude, if such a thing were ever his. As long as my mother does not hear of it I don't care about Moore's audacious act. All he wants, I know, is to make me angry and by my kicking up a row advertise it. I told him I rejoiced that he had cast the ring for me: one can only die once, and, as I am alive yet in spite of the oblivion he has provided, my name must do something now – it cannot die again!'

Tony Gray, in his biography of Moore – *A Peculiar Man* – provides a variation. Moore got the idea for his novel from an episode near Dublin at the time in which a former Catholic priest, who had become a Protestant clergyman, had abandoned his initial career, along with his clerical garb, when swimming across a lake to start a new life. By Gray's account Moore apprised Mrs Gogarty of his choice of name for the renegade prelate. Mrs Gogarty was predictably upset and made her feelings plain, whereupon Moore is said to have rejoined: "But, Madam, if you can supply a name with two such joyous dactyls I will change it."

To feature by name in one of George Moore's "outrageous" novels was a guarantee of publicity and notoriety in equal measure; and Oliver St John Gogarty was averse to neither. However, his awareness of his family's standing and his duty to uphold it he made clear in that same letter to Bell. "Yet it is annoying when I think how puzzled those who know me may be. There are so many relatives of mine nuns & religious that in Ireland it will be most unpleasant for me to be associated with the prototype – a Fr. Connellan – of the book who swam away from his parish [and who] is now proselytzing. Ireland is bigoted & the thing cannot fail to do me harm – the fact that I have nothing to do with it cannot avail."

George Moore's reckless larceny of Gogarty's name and – implicitly – his reputation, coincided with stirrings from another quarter. In Trieste in July Nora Barnacle gave birth to her son, Giorgio. Joyce immediately cabled Stannie: "Son born. Jim." Vincent Cosgrave, who emerges with little credit from this episode, added the words: "Mother and bastard doing well." He subsequently wrote to Joyce offering his congratulations, reporting that, "Gogarty has his M. B. at last and is now up for the Fellowship of the Surgeons . . . He takes a great deal of credit to himself about the success of the ménàge a Trieste the town of the Man of Sorrows." Warming to his task, Cosgrave continued on the topic of Gogarty. "At Christmas 'a stranger to you now' gave me the following little carol . . . The appended Song of J. is of course Gogarty's. He bids me send it. He desires you back in Dublin.'

If Gogarty had asked Cosgrave to forward "The Song of the Cheerful (but slightly sarcastic) Jaysus" to his erstwhile companion in exile as a peace offering, as Richard Ellmann contends, it would not gain acceptance as such in Trieste. Indeed, Cosgrave already knew this to be the case. Like George Moore, James Joyce was prepared to sacrifice his friends – and anyone else for that matter – to the cause of his literary art. Joyce had disclosed to both Stannie and Cosgrave that Stephen – in his novel *Stephen Hero* – would be portrayed as leaving Ireland as a result of the incident in the Martello Tower. Ellmann relates a conversation between the pair in July 1905 in which Cosgrave says: "I wouldn't like to be Gogarty when your brother comes to the Tower episode. Thanks be to God I never kicked his arse or anything."

CHAPTER SEVENTEEN

From the safety of his self-imposed exile in Trieste James Joyce was free to vent his spleen on those left behind, railing at *"inordinate wrongs,/ Imagined, outrageous,/Preposterous wrongs."*[1] His responsibilities as a family man had one immediately beneficial effect. He had to bring in sufficient to keep himself and his dependants, whether by his own efforts or those of the long-suffering Stannie. Joyce's physical remove also transformed Oliver Gogarty's progress, on several fronts. Relieved of Joyce's immediate influence, Gogarty finally applied himself to his medical studies, passing the first part of his Intermediate Medical Examination in the autumn of 1905 and the second part early the following year. His brother Henry had by then received his BA from Trinity College, being admitted to Kings Inns in the Hilary Term 1905. Richard, the youngest of the three Gogarty boys, had completed four years in Stonyhurst in December 1902, but did not go on to university.

Joyce's disappearance also regenerated Gogarty's nationalist sympathies. Under the pseudonyms "Alpha" and "Omega" he had continued to contribute political articles to Arthur Griffith's *United Irishman*. Now he took the floor at the first Annual Convention of the National Council of Sinn Fein, held in the Rotunda on Tuesday, 28 November 1905. The meeting was opened by the party president Edward Martyn, followed by Arthur Griffith, the founder of the party. Gogarty's hero propounded a policy of "national self-development through the recognition of the duties and rights of citizenship on the part of the individual, and by the aid and support of all movements originating within Ireland, instinct with national tradition and not looking outside Ireland for the accomplishment of their aims".[2]

Gogarty supported Griffith's motion, declaring: "There is yet in Ireland, in spite of extraordinary, persistent and pernicious attempts to crush it, an idea that we are in our own right entitled to be free and separate people." He gave it as his view that taxes levied to provide what was effectively mis-education; the Irish language was suppressed, Irish history ignored and the whole ethos concentrated on the might of the British empire. Exempted from this blanket condemnation were the Christian Brothers, whose qualities as educators and grasp of uniquely Irish cultural needs qualified them to teach not only at primary level, but at secondary level as well. In his analysis of third-level education Gogarty called upon his dual exposure to both Catholic and Protestant institutions.

"As regards a remedy for the University system, the first thing to be understood is that the difficulty of nationality is the most important: one has to identify himself mentally several times a day, and recall to mind to whom he belongs, if he would avoid being changed into one of those nationless nonentities such as the Universities of Ireland are tending to produce . . . the University should be for all classes without distinction, national from the very centre outwards."[3]

At the public meeting, roused by stirring performances from the St James's Brass Band and the York Street Brass Band, John Sweetman, Chairman of Meath County Council, proposed the following motion.

"That the people of Ireland are a free people, and that no law made without their authority or consent is or can ever be binding on their conscience." Gogarty rose to the occasion; neither on a point of order nor on the spur of the moment. "Now I do not rejoice to hear any man fume against England. But England assumes that most awful of responsibilities, that of governing a nation against her will."

Padraic Colum expressed the view that Gogarty at this time: "saw himself as a Roman, a man of the camp and the Senate, speaking a language of order and command." Others were less laudatory, notably the Trinity dons who had nurtured this nascent nationalist, unknowingly. A Trinity undergraduate was preaching sedition! Alarm, tinged with a sense of betrayal, prompted H. S. Macran, one of their number, to write to G. K. A. Bell expressing concern that the Trinity authorities might well feel obliged to take action against Gogarty if he did not modify his views. He could even be sent down. For his part, Gogarty put pen to paper to reassure his friend.

"So Makmeikan has been writing to you! My polemics are not dangerous: they are chiefly confined to articles in a weekly newspaper decrying the policy of sending members to parliament to get Home Rule which would deprive them of the livelihood they enjoy in the *getting* of it. We have no longer any State, no Athens now: but in order to build the City in my soul I exercise myself in writing against the palpable abuses of our time."

Another who saw senatorial material in the Trinity medical student was the very man who would one day appoint Gogarty to the upper house of the Free State Government. "My first connection with the National Movement was in 1905, when with my brother Phil and my uncle P. J. Cosgrave, I attended the first meeting of Sinn Fein presided over by Edward Martyn at the Rotunda, amongst those present being Dr. Oliver St. J. Gogarty." William Thomas Cosgrave must have been impressed by Gogarty's contribution on that occasion, for this recollection prefaced a deposition made by him almost half a century later, in which he emphasised that he had kept neither diaries nor records of the period in question.[5]

In the tumultuous year of 1906 – a watershed in Gogarty's life – he nevertheless found time to write of his concern for Dermot Trench, as he did to Dermot Freyer soon after a brief visit to England. "Poor dear old Trench: it would be a dreadful and for me irreparable calamity if anything happened to him. He overworks himself and troubles too much. How few of us value the best of all evangels. *'Consider the lilies of the field?'* I went out to consider them to-day. As there were none in the place I considered a wild cherry-tree instead. It was like a frozen fountain: all white bloom branched and sprayed like some tree on a white star might be. I could see the blue and the clouds up thro it as I lay supinely 'considering' it."

Earlier Gogarty had expressed similar concerns about Trench's mental condition to George Bell. "If I had an opportunity I could talk to and perhaps cheer a friend of ours – Trench – who is suffering and downcast latterly. His nerves are ailing and I am afraid he may shoot himself in a fit of despondency at the futility of his labours – pamphlets, etc."

Such fear was not unfounded, as Gogarty recalled in his "unpremeditated autobiography". "Trench's pamphlet, *What Is the Use of Reviving Irish*, is written in the clear style of a Balliol man. 'Gaelic is a language of social genius; its use reveals the Irishman to himself and sets in motion the genial current of soul that has become frozen in an Anglicised atmosphere. It is the symbol of a native social culture which was dignified and attractive in lieu of being snobbish and imitative, and for lack of which every man, woman and child in the country are denied their full expansion of personality.'

"Trench, with an enthusiasm which is the mark of madness, or of genius, or of both, made himself into a fluent Gaelic speaker. When he went back to Oxford he fell into the hands of one of those poverty-stricken, designing fellows who farm Oxford, on the lookout for Trenches and for their sisters who may make rich wives. The fellow that got hold of Trench married a titled woman and lived on her happily, for him, ever afterwards. Trench himself blew his brains out for the hopeless love of Lady Mary Spring-Rice."[6]

CHAPTER EIGHTEEN

Oliver Gogarty's career prospects had taken a definite turn for the better following James Joyce's departure. His results reflected that improvement, duly acknowledged by his mother. However, her health now began to deteriorate, thereby obliging her to take her errant eldest son into her confidence, after so many years of airy but determined dismissal and subjection. It may well have been, too, that Joyce's disappearance from the scene encouraged Margaret Gogarty to admit Oliver to that inner circle of family finance for so many years closed to him. It proved a baptism of fire, as he recounted in *Tumbling in the Hay*, under the appropriate chapter heading – "Transition".

Whereas Gogarty still awaited his examination results, Mr "Beddy" – his mother's trusted legal advisor – had now become a fully-fledged solicitor. As such, he proposed that Gogarty renounce his automatic right to his late father's estate, the latter having died intestate. The situation was further complicated by Mrs Gogarty's having continued to administer her late husband's estate, rather than put it into Chancery until Gogarty should have attained his majority. Happily, Mr "Beddy" was in a position to conceal that breach of the law, in return for Mrs Gogarty appointing him both trustee and residuary legatee. Mr "Beddy" emphasised the urgency for such action, particularly in the light of the rapid expansion of building development around the property that the late Dr Gogarty had acquired in Glasnevin.

Recourse to an independent solicitor offered Gogarty little comfort. "Has it occurred to you that in the unlikely event of your mother's death – that is, I trust it will be long delayed – neither you nor your brothers and sister, but your mother's solicitor would own this estate, which is rapidly increasing in value?"

To spare his mother any further anguish, Gogarty renounced all claim on his late father's estate.

In the aftermath of the libel suit that had arisen from *As I Was Going Down Sackville Street*, with its costly implications for both author and publisher, Constable must have been satisfied that the above episode recounted in *Tumbling in the Hay* did not constitute a libel before agreeing to publish it in 1939. It may well be that "Noll" Gogarty, who had acted for his father in the "Sackville Street" case, was able to satisfy Constable's legal advisors as to the accuracy and veracity of the circumstances outlined in the above excerpt. At any event, publication went ahead, successfully and without any injunction being sought.

Moreover, by that time tangible proof of Gogarty's claim existed in the form of a new road constructed off Botanic Road in the 1920s. During that decade Messrs Charles J. Reddy and Sons had received official approval for the construction of what became Fairfield Road, Glasnevin. By 1924 Messrs Reddy had erected 14 semi-detached houses on Fairfield Road, followed by four shops on the junction of Mobhi Road and Fairfield Road. Planning applications were in the name of the Reddy Estate, prompting Ruth McManus to note in *Dublin 1910-1940 – Shaping the City and Suburbs*. "While acting as solicitors in several cases where houses were sold by auction . . . Perhaps, like Mr [W. J.] Shannon, Reddy was a solicitor who acted as investor in construction projects."[1]

In May Gogarty alluded once again to his financial devastation when writing to Bell. "Truly I have had an adventurous week! One day I was in the heart of the country and the next in London. Very great friends of ours suffered heavily in the loss of San Francisco – $15,000 a year gone – and I was required to aid them in bearing the affliction! There are certain advantages in being born ruined; one is that pecuniary losses cannot affect overmuch."

A subsequent paragraph in that letter dated "May Day, 1906" assumes particular significance in the light of subsequent events. "How about your coming over to Ireland this summer? I will be altogether free after

June, and a week or a fortnight in the Tower would do you any amount of good. Sleep and poetry are the only possible activities. The sea makes one utterly unable to wound the wearied mind. Do consider it, and have it considered by the end of the month."

For a variety of reasons the Tower was to recede from Gogarty's lifestyle; one of the more bizarre being his wife's concern that he would contract fleas from the pigeons that frequented it. No record exists of his ever having entertained Bell in the Tower. However, one who continued to appreciate the recuperative properties of that eccentric refuge was Seumas O'Sullivan, as he wrote in acknowledgement of the loan of the premises. "The past week has been a perfect joy, bathing 2 or 3 times a day and lying in the sun, reading the remnants of the Tower Library and 'inviting my soul . . . these days have been a sort of resurrection of my first visit to Sandycove when I found you with that Oxonian Invalid trying to put into him some of the over-plus of your ever-abundant life."[2]

As with so many facets of Oliver St John Gogarty's picaresque progress through a crowded lifetime, the Martello Tower at Sandycove faded into the periphery of his existence. Tower No 11 was duly transferred from British to Irish control upon the creation of the Irish Free State, at which point Gogarty's lease, if still extant, presumably fell in and was not renewed under the new regime. Towards the end of his life Gogarty revisited his former abode, now inextricably linked both to him and to Joyce through *Ulysses*, and described obtaining the key from a son of Michael Scott, whose property the Tower had by then become. In ironic acceptance of life's twists and turns, Gogarty referred to it as "Joyce's tower".

CHAPTER NINETEEN

In 1906, the watershed year of Gogarty's life, issues arose so thick and fast that he can hardly have heard that Joyce had written to Stannie declaring that Gogarty would betray both Griffith and Sinn Fein. "No doubt whatsoever exists in my mind about this. It is my final view of his character, a native Irish growth."

Mixed fortunes in his medical examinations preceded a voyage to New York aboard the SS *Caronia*. By one account he travelled with "an old friend of his father's, Dick Burke of Fethard, Tipperary." In the light of subsequent family correspondence it seems more likely that the Dick Burke in question was a son of the famous Tipperary MFH, of whom Gogarty was to write at some length in *It Isn't This Time of Year at All!* in the chapter entitled "The Tipperary Hounds".

One possible explanation for what appears to have been a precipitate decision to cross the Atlantic only came to light many, many years later, when Paul Gogarty, the well-known travel writer and poet, finally decided to determine the truth of his purported lineage, as handed down to him through his father and grandfather. As it had been told to him, Paul's great-grandmother was called Mary Florence "Mayflo" Gogarty. She had eloped with a "writer", who had abandoned her on the birth of her infant son. In the circumstances Miss Gogarty had little option but to give the boy her own surname. This love child was subsequently reared by Oliver Gogarty's housekeeper, whom the boy was taught to regard as his surrogate mother. Little or nothing is known of Mayflo Gogarty's life prior to her marriage to Dr Roden Ryan, other than Noll Gogarty's observation that his aunt had had to leave the country in a hurry. And that disclosure was only coaxed from him when Noll was in his eighties. However, there is one reference in family correspondence to Mayflo having spent time with female cousins – both of them widowed – in Utica, New York. Moreover, Paul Gogarty's appearance and personality point strongly to his being a blood relation of Oliver Gogarty.

Gogarty was in New York when he wrote on 14 June from the Waldorf-Astoria Hotel. "Dear Joyce: I hope to be able to accept your kind invitation which you gave me as an alternative; I am making a tour of the world and I hope to be on the continent of Europe in the Autumn.

"I would much like to see Tokio – Yokogyo, Yokogyo, Yokogyo – but it is 17 days from San Francisco and the accommodation is not luxurious in that town just now. If I fail to afford to go far West to East you may see me in August, as I will be journeying to Italy then. I suppose I will be gladder to see you than you to see me: but I miss the touch of a vanished hand and the sound of a voice that is still."

Brenda, with her wistful smile, would occasionally recall her father's mischievous delight in laying false trails, creating smoke screens. This letter to Joyce is a perfect illustration. His initial proposition involved circumnavigating the globe from east to west. In the days before air travel, that was going to take months. On the other hand Gogarty proposed to be in Italy in August. The two schemes were hardly compatible. Instead of heading west Gogarty embarked on his return voyage aboard SS *Campania* on 27 June. He rekindled memories of that trip in a letter to his son-in-law fifty years later. "In 1906 I drove with [Peter F.] Collier in New York, in the back seat of his buggy. He had a curate or priest in the front seat 'to make his soul'. Peter Findlay Dunne sat in the back seat with me, the inventor of Dooley and Hennesey. Collier it was who put the first baths in Killeen Castle. I heard that from Lady Fingall."[1]

CHAPTER TWENTY

Unlike Joyce, who had experienced various infatuations before plumping for Nora Barnacle, Gogarty would not appear to have concerned himself with the fairer sex to any degree. His only admission of any such involvement is to be found in "Winifred", published in *Dana* in 1904.[1] Perhaps living with his mother, his aunt and his sister, in addition to his preoccupations with cycling, poetry, politics and his protracted medical studies, were reasons enough. There was a further consideration. He had relinquished his inheritance, and as yet had no profession. As such he was of limited attraction in the rigid social structure, with its inherent expectation of marriage that prevailed in Ireland at that time. Indeed, the only way that Oliver St John Gogarty could even contemplate marriage was by finding himself a woman with money of her own. Moreover, his mother, by virtue of obliging her firstborn to forgo his birthright, could scarcely demur. Gogarty was rising twenty-eight and the eldest son of a line not renowned for longevity.[2]

The precipitate nature of his courtship of Martha Duane and marriage to her suggests that she fulfilled those requirements. Two years Gogarty's senior, Martha Duane came of an ancient Connemara family and was then nursing in the Richmond Hospital,[3] where Gogarty was completing his practical education. At the time nursing was one of very few occupations considered appropriate to single women of genteel descent. Consequently it tended to be exclusively the domain of such ladies. Those responsible for the more menial tasks in the hospital wards were not classified as nurses. Moreover, Martha, like her mother-in-law, was a Galway girl, albeit "county" not "city".

Martha was the fourth of six children born to Bernard and Barbara Duane of Garranbaun, Moyard, County Galway. These Duanes had arrived in Connemara in the Middle Ages as stewards to the O'Flahertys and there remained ever since. The family motto *"Nulli praeda"* translates as "a prey for none". Dr MacLysaght in his *Surnames of Ireland* notes that the name "is usually anglicized Dwane in west Munster (also Divane in Kerry), Downes in Thomond, Duane in Connacht and occasionally Devane". He explains: "The majority of names beginning with *Dubh* or *Duibh* in Irish are derived from the adjective *Dubh*, black; the second part of such names is usually speculative being often obsolete forenames."

Perhaps the most renowned Duane of relatively modern times was James Duane (1733-1797), the first post-Independence Mayor of New York, controversial lawyer and property speculator. He was entrusted by George Washington with the reconstruction of the capital city – as New York was then – devastated by six years of war. James gave his name to both Duane Street and Duanesburgh. Although Martha claimed kinship with this successful entrepreneur, through a Bryan Duane, the biography of James Duane, *A Revolutionary Conservative*, does nothing to substantiate her claim.

Martha Duane, who was ever known as "Neenie", had come into money from outside her immediate family in 1905. Neenie spent much time up in County Mayo, in Cherry Cottage, on the Louisburgh road out of Westport, where the Rubie sisters, Mary and Martha, lived together, following the sudden death of their brother John. When William O'Brien, a native of Mallow, County Cork, political activist, founder and former editor of the *Irish People*, settled outside Westport with his wife to enjoy his retirement, they discovered that the middle-aged spinsters next door also had Mallow connections. Many years later William O'Brien's widow recounted the Rubie sisters' story, as told to her by a Westport priest. Their father, Michael, had been in line to inherit Mount Ruby, the ancestral estate outside Mallow. However, under the terms of his grandfather's will, he had disqualified himself by converting to Catholicism in accordance with his wife's wishes and the dictates of his conscience.

Thus impoverished, the Rubies moved to Dublin, where both Michael and his wife soon died, leaving their four orphaned children to be brought up by their great-uncle, Dean O'Rourke. John proved diligent, winning scholarships, whereas Bernard was idle, loathed schoolwork and eventually disappeared. After a number of years he renewed contact with his siblings, declaring that he had made good in America. On a return visit he had bought Cherry Cottage for his brother and sisters. As Bernard Rubie died unmarried – in Pittsburgh – and predeceased by brother John, he left the bulk of his considerable fortune to his surviving sisters. In the meantime Dean O'Rourke had prevailed upon the Rubie sisters to adopt as their own a foundling simply known as Nan, afterwards called Nannie O'Rourke. A handsome slice of Bernard Rubie's estate he also bequeathed to Neenie Duane, besides leaving £2,000 to the Convent of Mercy, Westport, for relief of the poor. A portion of this was used to purchase the property known as "Glendinnings" for conversion into a school. The connection between the Duane and Rubie families was of long standing, for a Mrs Rubie had stood as godmother to Teresa Duane, Neenie's eldest sister. The Rubie sisters never married. Mary died soon after Martha, joining her in the Rubie family vault in Aughavale cemetery south of Westport. Their fortune passed to Nannie O'Rourke, one of Neenie's closest friends.

And so it was that on Wednesday, 1 August 1906, Oliver St John Gogarty "medical student" of 5 Rutland Square and Fairfield, Glasnevin, married Martha "Neenie" Duane, spinster, of 17 Earlsfort Terrace in University Church, St Stephen's Green. The Rev. Fr. James P. Sherwin officiated, assisted by the Very Rev. Canon Canning, P.P., Ballyhaunis. The witnesses were John MacCabe and Eleanor Duane. John MacCabe, Gogarty's best man, would appear to have been the editor of *Dana*, to which Gogarty was an intermittent contributor. His brother F. F. "Freddie" MacCabe, racing manager to "Boss" Croker, was destined to gain racing immortality as the mastermind of Orby's victory in the 1907 Derby at Epsom, the first ever Irish-trained winner of the "Blue Riband". Eleanor "Nell" Duane, Neenie's youngest sister, became Mrs Robin Hunter and died in Arizona aged 87.

The honeymoon was celebrated initially in The Mitre, Oxford. The location impelled Gogarty – an inveterate letter writer whatever the circumstance – to resume his correspondence with Bell, suspended since his trip to America two months previously. "My dear Bell: We are putting in a few days here; and my wife is delighted with the place. I do not think we can possibly go to Wells however much as we desire it. It would take us a long way back and South too: here the heat is oppressive. South – what must it be? So we have relinquished the Innsbruck, Cortino, Venice programme. The highlands of Scotland & Donegal will be substituted; then to Connemara in September to stay with her people whom I have not as yet seen."

Instead, the honeymoon couple moved on to Teignmouth in Devon, over to Paris and ultimately down to Moyard in Connemara, where Gogarty met his wife's family for the first time. It was this first visit that also initiated Gogarty into what would become a lifelong enchantment with Connemara and the ever-changing colours of its rugged but beautiful landscape; lakes and mountains, sea and sky. The west of Ireland was to become a poetic muse – as in '*Connemara*'.[4]

There's something sleeping in my breast
That wakens only in the West;
There's something in the core of me
That needs the West to set it free.

Gogarty was delighted to discover that his father-in-law, Bernard Duane, then in his late sixties, was an American Civil War pensioner. He promptly won his father-in-law's approbation by refusing the local priest's demands for payment because Miss Duane had married outside her own parish and without his permission. This, of course, is not to suggest that the Duane family did not boast its share of "religious". Two of Bernard Duane's sisters, Margaret and Mary, had entered the Convent of Mercy in the nearby port of Clifden in 1864 and 1865 respectively. Margaret, the elder of the two, entered aged twenty, was duly professed as Sister Mary Regius in 1867 and lived out her days in the convent until her death in 1935, "'in the 71st year of her religious life", as the *Connacht Tribune* respectfully recorded. Mary, likewise professed in 1867 as Sister Mary Philomena, did not share her sister's longevity, dying in 1891.[5] Moreover, the Very Rev. Canon John T. Canning P.P., who had assisted at Neenie's wedding, had stood as godfather for Neenie's brother Matthias as long ago as June 1872 and would appear to have been related to the Duanes.

It was Nora Barnacle who alerted Joyce to Gogarty's altered status, holding out an Irish newspaper and exclaiming, "Guess the latest, guess who's married!" Joyce thought immediately of his brother Charlie, before deciding that this was yet another of Gogarty's practical jokes, as he had made no reference to impending nuptials in his correspondence. The fact that Joyce had not regularised his own union would have laid Gogarty open to further charges of treachery in his convoluted mind. Joyce subsequently observed to Stannie: "I fancy as he emerged from the church door his agile eye went right and left a little anxiously in search of a certain lean myopic face in the crowd, but he will rapidly grow out of that remaining sensitivity." On hearing that Gogarty had contributed pieces to Arthur Griffith's publications during his honeymoon, Joyce observed slyly: "Mrs Gogarty musn't have been very entertaining." Then, tiring of the topic, Joyce dismissed a postcard from Gogarty in Paris with the comment: "Of Gogarty's card I can make nothing. I don't understand why he desires that we should exchange short notes at long distances and at different angles to the equator." Nonetheless, Joyce did keep an eye on the newspapers for any announcement of the Gogartys' arrival in Italy on their honeymoon. The master of the "cryptogram" may have taken the reference in Gogarty's letter from New York in June to his visiting Italy in August as further evidence of Gogarty's deceit in concealing his plans to wed, in conformity with the Catholic church and Irish society.

Joyce summed up his current feelings about Gogarty in a letter to Stannie dated 3 December. "Explain how it is that while Byrne and Pappie and Mrs Cosgrave formed a true opinion of Oliver Gogarty, I, with more opportunity, formed an untrue one." While such sentiments imply that Joyce had renounced all friendship with Gogarty by this time, he was also fuelling Stannie's innate dislike of Gogarty.

The newlyweds moved into 17 Earlsfort Terrace, where Neenie's relations ran a select lodging house. Mrs Oliver St John Gogarty's calling card announced that they were "At Home Wednesdays in October". They can barely have settled in when Margaret Gogarty died on 29 December 1906 at her home in Rutland Square. The causes of death were certified as three years' suffering from chronic bronchitis and emphysema, leading to heart failure. Her death was witnessed and notified by Henry H. Gogarty, her son, who gave his mother's age as fifty-four. Little wonder that Gogarty should observe in *Tumbling in the Hay* that his was not a long-lived line.

In a letter to his older brother from The Grove, Fethard, where he was presumably enjoying hunting or shooting or both with his contemporary, Dick Burke, Henry Gogarty suggested that Oliver buy him out of whatever property still remained, in which Henry considered his shareholding free from all lien and therefore transferable. He further suggested that Oliver might either settle that portion of the property on his wife, or will it to her on his death.[6] The implication is quite clear. Gogarty would have to use his wife's inheritance to accomplish that proposed purchase, hence the advisability of settling it on her. Henry's readiness to divest himself of his share might be indicative of a decision to emigrate, as he was to do. In the absence of any similar suggestion apropos either Mayflo or Richard, their involvement remains unknown. Nevertheless, Mayflo, many years later, had property to dispose of in Glasnevin. At all events Oliver and Neenie Gogarty moved into Fairfield, where their first child was born on 23 July 1907 and duly christened Oliver Duane Odysseus Gogarty. Less than a month previously Gogarty had passed his final medical exams with second class honours.

In September the Gogartys took their infant son "Noll" to visit the Duanes in Garranbaun, in all likelihood by car, for as Gogarty related in his letter to Bell, he had been motoring since March. "Now that I am going away I would like to sell the car. If you know any wealthy fellow that wants a bargain double landaulette oh, speak!"

Leaving Noll in the care of Neenie's relations and a nurse in 17 Earlsfort Terrace, the Gogartys heading off to Vienna, the European capital of medical science. There he would further his specialist studies in Ear, Nose & Throat – otherwise rhinology – in the Allgemeines Krankenhaus under the acknowledged experts in that field, Hajek and Ottaker von Chiari. The aspiring specialist outlined his intentions in a letter to Dermot Freyer. Following six or nine months in Vienna, he proposed, "looking in at some of the London hospitals", where the services of a rhinologist might perhaps be appreciated.

The Gogartys took chambers in Vienna formerly occupied by Krafft-Ebing and the fledgling surgeon settled down to the grind of successive eight-hour days, handicapped by his lack of fluency in German. Tradition had it that the flag furled above the Krankenhaus should be flown, if a day passed without an inmate dying. Gogarty noted grimly that the flag never flew throughout his stay in Vienna. But he also recognised that innovative surgery, as practised there upon the destitute, involved frequently fatal degrees of trial and error. Years later, in faraway New Orleans, Stanley Gogarty, a cousin and garage proprietor, was upbraided by a doctor, whose automobile consistently gave trouble. Gogarty retorted: "Doctor, we fix our mistakes; you bury yours!"[7]

By the time Gogarty had completed the university research programme, which accompanied his stint in the hospital, all thoughts of practising in London had been dropped in favour of an immediate return to Dublin. In the interim repeated attempts to arrange a meeting with Joyce had come to nothing. One extract from a letter of Gogarty's to Joyce contrasts their fortunes, while at the same time making it quite plain that Gogarty is fully aware of the underlying cause of Joyce's intermittent illness.

"I heard you were stricken with a grievous distemper, and that you were paralysed. You can understand that the sight of your handwriting rejoiced me, as it disproved the statement that your right arm was paralysed. I was not a little surprised as well though the aetiology of a disease which your uncle insisted was altogether ethical should have prepared me for your miraculously being made whole again."

In hindsight it seems plausible that Joyce, guarded by the faithful Stannie, may have unwittingly gained an ally. It has frequently been observed that a woman's first stratagem, on getting married, is to identify and isolate those she considers undesirable among her husband's former cronies. Although unacquainted with James Joyce, Neenie cannot have been unaware of his reputation. Moreover, from the outset Neenie was assiduous in promoting her husband's medical career and boosting his reputation as an ENT specialist. That she could do in Dublin more effectively than in London. And it is likely that she knew her man well enough by now to realise just how fitful his dedication to a medical career might prove.

Neenie's misgivings were confirmed in her husband's letter to Seumas O'Sullivan dated 27 December 1907 in which he described himself as "about to return to the distasteful occupation of a Dublin surgeon amongst Dublin surgeons". The prospect strengthened his resolve to "kick hard for the last 3 weeks of liberty left before a life-time of respectability".

CHAPTER TWENTY-ONE

Oliver Gogarty, rhinologist, returned to his native city in March 1908, bringing with him the first bronchoscope ever seen in these islands, and his pregnant wife. He needed a hospital in which to employ the former, and a house in which to accommodate the latter, delighted as she was to be re-united with her firstborn, Noll. In the first instance Gogarty fell on his feet, for his return coincided neatly with Robert Woods' decision to confine his consultancy duties to Sir Patrick Dun's Hospital, thereby creating a vacancy at the Richmond Hospital, which Gogarty was only too pleased to be appointed to fill.

On the housing front Gogarty was equally happy to heed the advice of Sir Thornley Stoker, the eminent surgeon who lived in splendour in Ely House, the primary residence in Ely Place, a cul-de-sac to the east of St Stephen's Green. In emphasising the importance of a "good" address, Sir Thornley mentioned that the architect, Sir Thomas Deane, was anxious to find a buyer for 15 Ely Place, a Queen Anne style house with a verandah added, at the end of the cul-de-sac. Gogarty related the circumstances of his purchase in *It Isn't This Time of Year at All!*

"The next thing was to acquire a house. Sir Thornley Stoker, whom I consulted, advised me to take the house in which Sir Thomas Deane, the architect of the National Library and Museum, lived . . . It had a bronze Florentine knocker on the hall door and that decided me."

Not long after he had housed his family and attached himself to a hospital, Gogarty was struck down with appendicitis, a congenital failing. On that occasion eight days' bed-rest saved him from "Chirugery". However, the reprieve proved temporary. Later that year he was operated upon in the Elpis

(Greek for "hope") Private Hospital in Lower Mount Street. He described the episode in a letter to Dermot Freyer in characteristically fanciful language. "My dear Freyer: They have carried me kicking from my own house, muzzled me with alien airs [ether] and cut the appendix out of me!"

Meanwhile, Neenie was confined to bed in happier circumstances and in the comforting surroundings of her first real family home in the autumn, giving birth to her second son, Dermot St John, on Saturday, 5 September. Unlike Noll, who was always going to be dark-complexioned as his father was, Dermot took after his mother, being naturally fair-haired throughout his life. As Gogarty later wrote, "One son was brown, the other fair. All the forethought in the world could not have influenced Nature's bag when they were born sound and lively!"

As a committed pioneer of what was then called "automobilism", Gogarty declared, "I am going to drive myself into a practice." In so doing he was somewhat ahead of his time, in Ireland anyway. Despite the success of the Gordon Bennett race in 1903, car ownership in Ireland one year later was estimated at 213, whereas in Britain the motor population had swollen to 25,000. This overt but socially acceptable medium of advertising by medical men involved a progression from a 20hp Argyll, through a Mercedes, eventually to a buttercup-coloured Rolls-Royce, reputedly the first of its kind in the capital. These he frequently drove himself, attired in fur motoring coat and top hat. However, he was being driven by his chauffeur when his car crashed in Bray, killing a child. That tragedy occurred in July 1909, and Gogarty sought escape from his grief by crossing to London later that month to attend a celebration dinner for Louis Bleriot, who had made the first cross-channel flight on 25 July. That particular foray saw him blow £100. Happily for him and his family, £100 meant little one way or another, such was the society clientele that was being directed to 15 Ely Place, initially through referrals from Sir Thornley Stoker, "who had a rich and fashionable practice, saw to it that I remained solvent in Ely Place."[1]

Gogarty's return from London coincided with James Joyce's first visit to his native city since his clandestine departure with Nora Barnacle almost

five years before. The first figure that the purblind exile identified on
Kingstown pier was "Gogarty's fat back." Joyce promptly took evasive
action. Besides bringing his young son Giorgio to meet his relatives, Joyce
was intent on reaching agreement with Maunsell & Co. for the publication
of *Dubliners*. While Joyce may not have been prepared for such a sudden
encounter, he can hardly have expected that, in a town as small as Dublin
was then, his erstwhile friend would remain long in ignorance of his return.
Duly the summons arrived at 44 Fontenoy Street, where Joyce and Giorgio
were staying with the patriarch, John Stanislaus Joyce. It was dated 31, VII.
'09 – a Saturday.

"Dear Joyce: Curiosis Cosgrave tells me you are in Dublin. Before trying
to get you to come to lunch at Dolphin on Monday next at 1.0'c I would
like to have a word with you. My man will drive you across (if you are in).
I leave town at 5 each evening; but there can be changes if you turn up.

"He will call about 3.20. Do come if you can or will. I am looking forward
to seeing you with pleasure. There are many things I would like to discuss
and a plan or two to divert you. You have not yet plumbed all the depths
of poetry; there is Broderick the Bard! Of whom more anon. Yours, O. G."

That particular arrangement was subsequently cancelled due to a
professional consultation. "Dear Joyce: I find that 1 o'c. tomorrow there
is a patient coming who cannot come at any other time. I will be glad
if, in view of this, you will forgive a little postponement of the lunch. I
will let you know. Yours, O. G." Gogarty dated that note 2. VIII. '09.
However, elementary detective work indicates that this second note was
despatched on Sunday, 1 August, if only to tie in with the unalterable
consultation to which it refers, being Monday, 2 August. Further delving
in Gogarty's casebook for the period identified the inflexible patient as one
Mr McCabe, of whom the consultant, in typically indecipherable medical
scrawl, noted "Never deaf", and "Prescribed – drops to rub in behind ear".

It was apparently by chance that the pair encountered in Merrion Square,
where Joyce once again tried to evade Gogarty. The latter was not to be so
lightly brushed aside, grabbing Joyce and declaring, "Jaysus, man, you're
in phtisis." It was hardly the most reassuring observation, for "phtisis" is

defined as a progressive wasting disease that can incorporate the dreaded and frequently fatal tuberculosis. Reluctantly, Joyce allowed himself to be brought back to 15 Ely Place, where he steadfastly refused any form of hospitality, stating baldly, "You have your life, leave me to mine."

"Well, do you really want me to go to hell and be damned?"

"I bear you no ill-will. I believe you have some points of good nature. You and I of six years ago are both dead. But I must write as I have felt."

"I don't care a damn what you say of me as long as it is literature."

"Do you mean that?"

"I do, honest to Jaysus! Now will you shake hands with me at least?"

"I will, on that understanding."[2]

That was Joyce's account of what was to prove his final meeting with Gogarty, as he reported back to Stannie in Trieste, anxious to reassure his doting brother of his resistance to any of Gogarty's blandishments, although "phtisis" could hardly be classified as complimentary. Moreover, had Joyce been aware of Mary Fleming's description of the sensation of shaking hands with him, he might well have altered his account. Mary, an elderly cousin of J. F. Byrne, "disliked Joyce, partly because, 'When he holds out his hand for you to shake, you feel nothing but five little, raw, cold sausages.' And Joyce did not like Mary. And that is why in his *Ulysses*, Mrs. Fleming is the lady who cooks and darns socks for Poldy and Molly Bloom in number 7 Eccles Street."[3]

Gogarty's recollection of that final encounter with Joyce was, not surprisingly, somewhat at variance. By his account Joyce arrived around to Ely Place on foot and was duly admitted to an enthusiastic reception, which he failed to reciprocate. Declining all offers of tea, or coffee, or something stronger and dismissing an invitation to accompany his host to Enniskerry to meet Mrs Gogarty, Joyce all the while stared silently out a window at a colourful, luxuriant display of roses in the garden beyond. After a prolonged interval Joyce abruptly asked, "Is this your revenge?" Perplexed, Gogarty asked for elucidation. "On the public," was Joyce's enigmatic response, whereupon he took his leave.

In his appraisal of this, Gogarty's final encounter with Joyce, Richard

Ellmann accepted unreservedly Joyce's version, though his grounds for saying that Joyce declared his intention to incorporate the Martello Tower episode in his novel are not apparent. His observation, "Joyce's coolly announced intention of describing the tower episode put Gogarty in some trepidation", is suggestive of blackmail. True, Joyce did content himself by noting that Gogarty "fears the lancet of my art as I fear that of his." However, that does not constitute proof positive of Joyce's avowed intention to make reference to the goings on in the tower. Instead, it lays open to conjecture precisely what did take place in the tower during that fateful night of 15 September 1904.

As it transpired, Joyce had little opportunity to gloat on that occasion, for Vincent Cosgrave was quick to sow the seeds in Joyce's receptive mind of Nora's infidelity with him. Allowing Cosgrave's claims to run riot in his mind, Joyce sought out J. F. Byrne, who described their encounter in *Silent Years*.

'Joyce had good reason to remember No. 7 Eccles Street, for it was to that house one subsequent afternoon that he came, in a state of utter perturbation, to see me. He told me of something that had just occurred to him in Dublin. Of this "something" I will not say more than it was not related to either his literary work or his business efforts. I had always known that Joyce was highly emotional, but I had never before this afternoon seen anything to approach the frightening condition that convulsed him. He wept and groaned and gesticulated in futile impotence as he sobbed out to me the thing that had occurred. Never in my life have I seen a human being more shattered, and the sorrow I felt for him then and my sympathy were enough to obliterate forever some unpleasant memories. I spoke to him and succeeded in quieting him; and gradually he emerged *de profundis*. He stayed for dinner and supper and spent the night in my house. The following morning he was up early, fully out of the gloom, and after breakfast he went off, humming as he went.

"In the late afternoon of the same day he returned, and with almost childlike pleasure he opened a little jewel box to show me a trinket he had bought for Nora. It consisted of five matched pieces of ivory, each about half an inch in diameter; they were strung on a gold chain and made a beautiful and uncommon token. 'It's beautiful,' I said, 'you got one ivory for each year you've been with her.' 'I never thought of that,' he admitted frankly, 'but it's a splendid idea; and I'll add one to it every year.'"[4]

Frank Delaney was less circumspect, getting straight to the heart of the matter, free from the constraints of friendship and discretion that John Francis Byrne clearly felt bound by, even though withholding publication until after both Joyce and Nora had gone to their reward.

Byrne rallied and railed. Unlike Joyce, he hadn't left Dublin and had kept pace with the city's sense of jealousy and conspiracy. He soon smelt what had happened, that the story of Nora's infidelity was in fact a vengeful plan hatched by the envious Cosgrave and viciously encouraged by Gogarty. Subsequently Nora – who had behaved quietly and with dignity under such swingeing accusations – confided in Joyce's brother, Stanislaus, who was able to confirm Byrne's assessment. Cosgrave had previously admitted to Stanislaus his failure to oust Joyce from Nora's heart. It was never difficult to convince Joyce that people were conspiring against him and his relief was so complete that he commemorated Nora's fidelity by immortalising Number Seven, Eccles Street.'[5]

Vincent Cosgrave was to receive his "reward" for blackening Nora in Joyce's eyes by being portrayed as "Lynch" – the Judas, the betrayer – in *Ulysses*. In the meantime, lest he should forget, Joyce entered this description of Cosgrave in one of his ever-present notebooks. "The long slender flattened skull under his cap brought up the image of a hooded reptile: the eyes, too, were reptilian in glint and gaze but with one human point, a tiny window of a shrivelled soul, poignant and embittered."[6] Like Gogarty, his alleged co-conspirator, Cosgrave never saw Joyce again. But, unlike Gogarty, Cosgrave would not long outlive his portrayal in *Ulysses*.

Wittingly or otherwise, J. F. Byrne, in allaying Joyce's paranoid suspicions of Nora, confirmed the latter's estimation of Gogarty's villainy and malice toward him. If any lingering vestiges of loyalty to Gogarty had existed before their final encounter, they had now been swept away. Joyce was free to vilify Gogarty in any way he saw fit, short of libelling his sometime friend and benefactor. Nor was Gogarty's usefulness to be confined to "Buck Mulligan". He would also serve as the model for "Doherty" in *Stephen Hero* and "Robert Hand" in *Exiles*. Moreover, elements of Gogarty are held to appear in "Ignatius Gallagher", "Jimmy Doyle" and "Lenehan" in *Dubliners*.

CHAPTER TWENTY-TWO

Ellmann, in dealing with the friendship between Gogarty and Joyce and its decline into estrangement, contended that the pair had fought a duel for literary mastery in which Gogarty suffered humiliation. J. B. Lyons, an infinitely more equitable observer of the human condition, took the view that the two young men had simply outgrown one another, going their separate ways, content to follow each other's career at a geographical and emotional remove. Constantine Curran, a contemporary and friend of both, observed that Joyce had made his alienation plain in his "epiphany", written before he went into exile, whereas Gogarty remained ostensibly well disposed, until the publication of *Ulysses*.

Their different paths through life may have contributed to their contrasting attitudes to one another. Whereas Joyce felt it necessary to stay far away from the only place about which he was ever to write, Gogarty plunged into his profession, while also making time to write and to become increasingly embroiled in Arthur Griffith's Sinn Fein movement for national self-determination. On the professional front Oliver St John Gogarty was conferred with Fellowship of the Royal College of Surgeons in Ireland on 19 March 1910, and subsequently with membership of the Royal Society of Medicine.

Within twelve months of becoming FRCSI Gogarty applied for the position as ENT surgeon in the Meath Hospital, where such a vacancy arose on the resignation of Mr Conway Dwyer. Of course, it wasn't just so straightforward, as Gogarty was later to recount in his "unpremeditated autobiography".

In this instance Gogarty makes light of the situation that existed in those days, long before the Welfare State was more than a socialist vision.

Surgeons and physicians treated those who could not pay in the morning, and recouped the cost of their time and skill in the afternoon, courtesy of those who could afford their services. When Gogarty, an ENT specialist, remarked that he made his afternoon patients pay through the nose he meant it in more ways than one. For all of that, there are those who recall with affectionate appreciation his intercession to obtain for them specialist treatment otherwise way beyond their means or access.

That shuttle between the Richmond and the more lucrative Meath, with Conway Dwyer completing the switch in reverse, came at an opportune time for the younger man. On 2 March 1911 Neenie gave birth at home in Ely Place to her third and final child, a daughter, duly christened Brenda Martha. Brenda, the golden haired subject of "Golden Stockings", would insist in later years that she had been born in 1912; lukewarm proof of Oscar Wilde's humorous observation that a woman who will tell you her age will tell you anything. However, Brenda's little subtraction was nothing when compared to the fiction in which her mother engaged when Free State passports were first issued. In siring a family of three Oliver Gogarty proved the most prolific of his siblings. Henry never married, Mayflo had one legitimate daughter and Richard likewise.

Dr Peter Gatenby, Physician to the Meath Hospital half a century later, recorded Gogarty's switch of hospitals in his history of the Meath and paid him the following tribute, albeit in more balanced measure.

During this period of tension, two appointments of interest were made by the medical board, though there was no specific confirmation of these in the minutes of the joint committee. Oliver St John Gogarty was elected as surgeon in February 1911. He filled the vacancy made by the retirement of Conway Dwyer, professor of surgery at the Royal College of Surgeons, who transferred to the Richmond Hospital. Gogarty was the first ear, nose and throat surgeon appointed to the Meath. His particular expertise was the treatment of sinusitis, and he also recognised the importance of draining an unsuspected collection of pus in the maxillary antrum. Gogarty became best known for his brilliant literary ability, which completely overshadowed his medical career and his remarkable life has been fully described in the biographies by Ulick O'Connor and J. B. Lyons. He was a brilliant conversationalist, poet and wit, and author of *Tumbling in the Hay* and *As I Was Going Down Sackville Street*, and many other publications. He was also a senator in the first senate of the Irish Free State. He was notably the first Catholic to obtain a senior appointment at the Meath in the twentieth century.[1]

At the time of Gogarty's appointment the Meath Hospital maintained a tradition whereby a senior member of the staff gave an address at the opening of the Winter Session. Abandoned at the outbreak of WW1, this custom was revived during WW2. In 1911 Gogarty took as his subject "The Need of Medical Inspection of School Children". He placed his emphasis on prevention being more important than cure.

Gogarty identified the symptoms he encountered in his daily practice to underline his case for prevention as opposed to cure. They included mouth-breathing, facial disfiguration and pigeon-chest, products of long, hungry hours of school attendance on already under-nourished youngsters. "Torturing with teaching a little starving child affects both the mind and body." He can only have inspired incredulity amongst his listeners when calling for the provision of school meals, before exhorting his audience with characteristic rhetoric: "These children are the Nation of to-morrow. Save it!"[2]

Doubtless dismissed by many at the time as a pious wish, Gogarty's appeal for the provision of school meals was to bear fruit some three years later, if to a qualified extent. On 10 August 1914 the Education (Provision of Meals) (Ireland) Act was entered on the statute books. It empowered – though it did not compel – local authorities to provide meals for schoolchildren.

Besides his laudable, if somewhat controversial preoccupation with the efficacy of preventative measures in the context of contemporary practices, Gogarty also paid homage to his own medical provenance, as E. P. Scarlett noted many years later. "But finally I was satisfied that he was not a myth but a person when on a subsequent visit to the historic Meath Hospital, Dublin, I talked with his medical colleagues and noted a plate on an oval table in the medical Board Room indicating that Oliver Gogarty had presented the table in memory of his father, Dr. Henry Gogarty."

CHAPTER TWENTY-THREE

Seldom one to dwell on chapters in his life that he considered closed, Gogarty seems to have put Fairfield out of his mind once moving to Ely Place. At all events there is no further reference to the Glasnevin property by name following the move into that fashionable cul-de-sac off St Stephen's Green, where Gogarty's neighbours included George Moore, Henry Lionel Barnardo, the well known furrier and, of course, the redoubtable Sir Thornley Stoker. For all his eminence at the time, the last named was destined to be overshadowed in posterity by his brother, Abraham "Bram" Stoker, creator of Dracula. Curiously, both brothers died in 1912, when Sir Thornley's treasure trove of antiques, often extracted from patients in lieu of fees, came up for auction, with Gogarty among the purchasers. George Moore had abandoned Dublin in favour of London for what proved the final time a year previously.

It was through that auction that Gogarty subsequently became acquainted with his contemporary Lord Dunsany, whose agent, Colonel Hammond, had been despatched to recover a treasured vase, extracted from Dunsany Castle by Sir Thornley Stoker by way of payment. The Gogartys were duly invited to a ball in the castle. Bored with the formalities, Gogarty sought somewhere quiet, only to find himself in the company of his similarly reticent host.

While it was in full swing I wandered through the passages searching for some place where I might sit in quiet and get, if necessary, the spirit of the thing, without the action, for I am strangely averse to group enjoyments of any kind. At last I found a settee in a corridor on one end of which a tall youth was seated biting a fingernail. His hair was fair, his forehead extraordinarily high, noble and unfurrowed. His mouth, which a light moustache left unconcealed, was imperious with a clear chin line under a cold beauty of eyes and brow. He looked as if he belonged to a race aloof, exempt from the pathos of the common concerns of mankind.

"I took a seat beside him for there was none other to be had . . . I had quoted almost all Herrick's *Hesperides* and was about to start on his *Nook Numbers*, when someone drew my audience away."[1]

That account was quoted by Mark Amory from Gogarty's unpublished essay on the man who was to become his lifelong friend. Amory went on to point out that Gogarty, for all his conflicting characteristics as busybody, gossip and occasional troublemaker, endeared himself to Dunsany through his kindness, his quickness of wit and his capacity to amuse. So much so that Dunsany would entertain Gogarty's risqué stories, whereas Shane Leslie's attempts in similar vein saw Dunsany having recourse to reading a book; a sign of his displeasure. "Gogarty remained on good terms with almost everyone almost all the time, no easy feat over the next twenty years in Dublin."[2]

The friendship of two kindred spirits was tested on occasion by Gogarty's sense of mischief, with his fellow poet and playwright as its butt. Dunsany was content to bide his time, as he wryly recorded in his memoirs. At Gogarty's instigation Dunsany allowed himself to be inveigled into taking part in the chess competition in the Tailteann Games.

"But now I entered for the Major Tournament. I think I may have been partly goaded to do it because, when Gogarty had without telling me and out of pure kindness entered one of my books for another competition in the Tailteann Games, and, being always closely in touch with what was going on in Dublin, told me that I was going to get the first prize, a man with more influence than Gogarty, but less generosity, had got to hear of it, and I got neither first, second nor third prize nor a mention. It may have been then that in a moment of petulance I said, 'I will enter for something the result of which he cannot possibly control.'

"All of the rest I had now beaten except Mr. Varian, whom I had still to play, and whom rumour made out to be the most redoubtable. If I drew with him I should still win the tournament, but if I lost I should be only equal with him and Mr. Orr, and I was very much afraid of him until we started playing. He played with extraordinary brilliance, and almost immediately had a great advantage, but I said to myself, 'This is unsound', and I sat and waited for what I thought was his eccentric opening to break down. It did not, however, break down, and it was a long time before I was able to turn the tables and finally win. This easily gave me the first prize, and a silver-gilt medal with the head of Queen Tailtea on it, who has been dead too many thousand years for me to know if it is like her. I went first to Gogarty's house, who also had a party for the Horse-Show, and found his kindness, which can always be relied on, ready with sympathetic words of condolence; but, when he found they were not needed, I found this brilliant conversationalist for the first time in my life without very much to say."[3]

Dunsany had made plain his dislike of W. B. Yeats years previously, to the extent of refusing to submit further plays to the Abbey after 1911, feeling the Yeats and Lady Gregory favoured their own productions to the detriment of his works. Nor can Yeats have helped their relationship by quoting Lady Gregory, while staying in Dunsany Castle: "It is good for you to stay with simple well-bred people." Unaware that the Dunsanys knew her remark to have been about themselves, Lady Gregory later compounded the insult by quoting her own remark in full. "It is good for you to stay with simple well-bred people, they need not be clever."

Gogarty gave his views on this animus in his unpublished essay on Dunsany. "It would be a mistake to think that the rivalry between Dunsany and Yeats was a literary one. Far from it. Yeats had no rival to fear among contemporary poets. It was not so much rivalry on Yeats' part (shocking to say it before it can be explained) as it was envy. Yeats, though his descent was from parsons, dearly loved a lord. He was at heart an aristocrat, and it must always have been a disappointment to him that he was not born one. Not by taking thought could he trace his descent from the year 1181 . . . This then was at the bottom the cause of the failure between Dunsany and Yeats. Dunsany sensed some sort of opposition, real and imaginary for some of the forms it was reputed to have taken were probably part of an over sensitive suspicion."[4]

While he made no attempt to force Gogarty to side with him in his antipathy to the "arch-poet", neither did he hesitate to poke fun at Gogarty's admiration of Yeats, as well as Gogarty's dislike of field sports. "I wrote a few more poems in August, and that year my gamekeeper, James Toomey, succeeded in luring a flight of ducks to a pond. He had been at it for some time, but now his efforts were so successful that in two flights that month I shot thirty, and in later years the flight was even better. I went to see Gogarty in the house that he had built on an island in a Galway lake, perhaps influenced by Yeats's nine bean rows, and then we went to Kildalton, where I shot two stags, one of them a royal, besides black game, grouse and others of the many things that may be shot at that lovely place."[5]

The island house – inspired, as Gogarty would later confirm, by Yeats's "Isle of Inisfree"' – still stands on Heather Island, Tully Lake, Renvyle. Dunsany commemorated his visit in the form of one of his characteristic odes, written on parchment with a quill pen and dedicated to his host. Gogarty was to reflect upon that Yeats connection in *Rolling down the Lea*. Heather Island he called "Freilaun", its Gaelic name. "When I think that the poet Yeats spent a night on a rock beside Lough Gill gazing through the midnight glimmer at Inisfree, which he was never to reach to build his cabin, and of the years through which he longed in vain for his love, it is disturbing to know that the best poetry comes from a longing that must be forever unfulfilled. Yet here I am where I longed to be. All that I can do with my ease is to weave some light rhymes together about the passing away of comely things . . ."[6]

In his biography of Gogarty, Ulick O'Connor recorded that Fairfield, in which W. B. Yeats resided for a while in 1910[7], was sold in 1912[8]. It was subsequently replaced in the Gogarty property portfolio by Renvyle House in faraway, enchanting Connemara. Much more recently Robert O'Byrne, in his engrossing biography of Hugh Lane, the famously controversial art dealer, alluded to Lane's brief flirtation with buying a house in Ireland, principally at the instigation of his doting aunt, Lady Gregory. Gogarty had been acquainted with the formidable Augusta Gregory for more than a decade and would later write plays for "her" Abbey Theatre, as well as becoming her medical consultant. Hugh Lane discounted his aunt's suggestion that he take what had been George Moore's house in Ely Place. Rather did he respond quite positively to Gogarty's showing him Delville, originally Dr Delaney's residence in Glasnevin. Delville had later belonged to Sir Patrick Keenan, an uncle of Lady Fingall's. In her memoirs, *Seventy Years Young*, Daisy Fingall described her wedding reception in Delville on 15 May 1883, following the religious ceremony in the Archbishop of Dublin's private chapel in Rutland Square. "The Viceroy and Lady Spencer and all the Viceregal Court, of course, were there. And an enormous number of guests . . . Our going-away carriage came to the door drawn by the traditional white horses of the Plunketts." While Gogarty's promotion of the house in Glasnevin might suggest that Fairfield was Delville by another name, such was not the case. Most likely it was Delville's literary and artistic associations that prompted his advocacy of it as an appropriate residence for one of Lane's pretensions. In the event Hugh Lane continued to reside in London, despite seeking and securing the post of Director of the National Gallery of Ireland.

As he said himself, Gogarty met all types through his medical practice, Hugh Lane, "picture dealer", being one. William Orpen, "portrait painter" and Gogarty's contemporary, was another. Later to become the most highly paid society portraitist in these islands, Orpen painted Gogarty in 1911. The two became friends, often escaping from the noise and bustle of the city to savour a refreshing hour or so in "Lamb" Doyle's public house in the foothills of the Dublin mountains, enjoying the views clear across the city to the Hill of Howth in the distance, with Dublin Bay in between. Besides incorporating Gogarty in his well known painting "The Café Royal" in 1912, Orpen also painted a full length portrait of the young Noll Gogarty. Exhibited in the Royal Hibernian Academy in 1913, it was donated to the National Gallery of Ireland prior to Noll's death in 1999.

Bruce Arnold, in his biography of Orpen, made no bones about one basis at least for his subject's friendship with Gogarty, describing the latter as a "womaniser". Both, however were zealous in guarding their wives' virtue, to the extent that Neenie never met Orpen, and Grace

Orpen met Gogarty rarely, if at all. Having thus tarnished Gogarty's reputation in a way that neither of his own biographers had seen fit to do, Arnold then redressed the situation somewhat when adding that the two did not find communion so much in women as in drink. His qualification was timely, for otherwise the pair ran the risk of being doubly damned as "Irish queers" – Irishmen who rate the pleasures of the flesh more highly than alcohol!

Orpen was additionally attracted by Gogarty's Rolls Royce, which the latter purchased in the autumn of 1910[9]. The buttercup yellow monster was accompanied by its chauffeur-cum-mechanic, nineteen-year-old Joshua Barr, incongruously a member of the Plymouth Brethren. In due course Orpen realised his ambition in this respect, when acquiring his own Rolls Royce in 1914, at which point he employed Joshua Barr, whom Gogarty had let go the previous year with this qualified reference, for a chauffeur. "He is sober, honest but unpunctual."

While Bruce Arnold may have wished Orpen kept safely away from Neenie Gogarty, such total segregation could hardly have proved feasible in the context of the literary salons that had become the fashion of the day in the cradle of the Irish renaissance that was Dublin. AE, Yeats, Sarah Purser and Stephen McKenna all had their specific days of the week on which to play host to the great and the good of the Irish cultural revival and its concurrent political aspirations. McKenna went so far as to encourage his visitors to converse in either Irish or Greek. No such restrictions were imposed on visitors to 15 Ely Place, where Neenie played hostess to her husband's friends and acquaintances on Friday evenings. The young and impressionable Marquess of Conyngham, delighted at his inclusion for all his lack of years and erudition, listed off some of those he met under the Gogartys' roof. They included the Yeats brothers, Jack and Willie, Augustus John, Lord Dunsany, Sir Horace Plunkett, Daisy Lady Fingall and William Orpen[10].

CHAPTER TWENTY-FOUR

Posterity owes a considerable debt to one Joseph Holloway for his impressions of Dublin in the first quarter of the twentieth century and Dublin theatre in particular. By his own account: "Dublin without its Abbey would be a very dull place indeed for me!" His diary entry for Thursday, 10 July 1913 provides a taste.

"When I was downtown in the early part of the day, I saw 'AE' looking into Greene's library window and scanning the backs of the books with his nose nearly touching the glass. He was looking well and more tidy than usual. He had discarded his old overcoat, and had his hair and beard trimmed. Dr. Gogarty motored past with a lady in the motor, as I stood at the door of No. 6, St. Stephen's Green, and I thought of George Moore's description of him in *Salve* as the wit of Dublin. To me he always looks like an overgrown schoolboy who would like to be thinner so that he could more readily take part in games."

The kindly theatre buff might not have known, but Gogarty had "games" enough on his plate, even for one of his versatile talents. Through his hospital practice Gogarty had become increasingly vociferous in his campaign to eradicate what he considered the major cause of disease in Dublin – the notorious slums to the north east of the Liffey. The death rate in Dublin in 1913 exceeded that of both Moscow and Calcutta. Ironically, the worst conditions prevailed in what had once been the most exclusive area of the city, effectively abandoned by the great and the good following the Act of Union in 1800. One witness, testifying at a Government enquiry in 1913, described a single tenement house in which no fewer than 107 people were living, in conditions of utmost squalor and human degradation. *The Irish Times* went so far as to liken the Dublin slums to Dante's "Inferno".

That same year Gogarty delivered an address to the Academy of Medicine, entitled "On the Inspection of Dublin school children" echoing his speech two years before in the Meath Hospital.

"In the poorest districts only about half the children bring even a piece of bread with them and when at 3:30 they return the family dinner is over. The breadwinners of the family have very naturally eaten any meat that may be there and little is left for the children but bread and tea . . . Hundreds of children are literally starving in the schools and we cannot get the Irish M.P.s to pay the slightest attention or to get the free meal for children, which provides feeding for children in England, Scotland and Wales, extended to Ireland."

Gogarty also emphasised the necessity for clean milk and fresh air. The streets, he said, were full of mud and manure, "dust and dessicated dung that pervaded houses and utensils." Sanitation, he held, was well-nigh non-existent. A letter in the same vein conveyed his sense of outrage.

"Does a tenement only cease to be a tenement, when it becomes a tomb? The houses in Church Street, as elsewhere, have the saving attribute of killing only one generation or part of a generation . . . but what of the houses on Church Street, the houses of six and seven feet high, that cannot fall, but can only go on reeking forever. The houses in Kean's Court – what of those? And what of those structures in Thunder's Court, where the one common privy bemerded beyond use, stands beside the one common water supply which a corporation notice guards from waste."[1]

His address was duly reported in *The Irish Times* the following day, evoking praise from, among others, Maud Gonne, then involved in social work in the city. However, Gogarty had already begun to realise that polemic alone would not carry the day. Satire, he was obliged to concede, had a negative effect when delivered as a straightforward oration. A more dramatic metier was required, where humour could be used to sugar the pill, lull the unwary, incense the indifferent. His thoughts turned to the theatre, specifically to the Abbey. As *Blight – the Tragedy of Dublin* began to take shape in Gogarty's sometimes hyper-active mind, similar stirrings, though of a more ruminative and deliberate nature, were taking place in distant Trieste.

James Joyce had made a further return visit to Ireland in the summer of 1912. Nora had taken their daughter, Lucia, back home to meet her family, whereupon Joyce set off in impromptu, precipitate pursuit with young son Giorgio. This undignified behaviour prompted Nora to write "after all our little squabbles he couldn't live without me for a month." The other purpose of Joyce's return visit was to stir the publisher George Roberts – Maunsel & Company – into going ahead with *Dubliners*, on which he had been sitting for ten months. While negotiations dragged on Joyce was introduced to James Stephens, whom Joyce described to his brother as "my rival, the latest Irish genius." For all of that, or perhaps because of it, he quarrelled with the affable Stephens. Arthur Griffith proved more supportive, and duly received recognition of that support by laudatory mention in *Ulysses*. After characteristic procrastination Roberts refused to proceed with *Dubliners*, as did the intended printer, John Falconer. Worse still, Falconer shredded what copies he had already printed. On his gloomy, penniless journey back to Trieste, Joyce wrote *Gas from a Burner*, a diatribe against those who stood between him and his avowed objective: "to forge in the smithy of my soul the uncreated conscience of my race."

Then thirty years old, James Joyce could have been forgiven had he followed his own advice to James Stephens: to give up writing and take up some more promising profession, such as shoe shining. In the three years since his final encounter with Gogarty, Joyce had made no progress in his literary career, rather had he found every door closed in his face because he would not write other than what he felt impelled to write. And that writing was offensive to arbiters of good taste, moral guardians and all right-thinking Irishmen. Moreover, the income from journalism by which he purported to keep his family, while crafting literary masterpieces, was manifestly inadequate. To make matters worse, he wanted to write only about his native city and the denizens of "dear, dirty Dublin". For material to this end Joyce depended on family and his few remaining friends in Dublin to supply him with news from afar.

As a consequence of his natural flamboyance and his need to finance what was an extravagant lifestyle, Gogarty was seldom out of the news from home. Such reports can have done little to soothe the savage breast that beat with anger and frustration in Trieste. Resent his former friend and benefactor as he might, Joyce could not escape the knowledge that he had once elected to qualify in medicine specifically to fund his literary aspirations. Was Gogarty to succeed in treading that very path through medicine to literary renown? Even without being prey to the paranoia that dogged him all his life, Joyce would have been less than human had he not succumbed to one of the greatest and most enduring failings of his race – begrudgery.

All the while political tensions continued to mount, fuelled by blatant gun-running into Ulster ports; a declaration of intent by the Unionists to resist any attempts by Westminster to confer Home Rule on Ireland. Inevitably, that example was duplicated further south, with Erskine and Mary Childers defying the elements and coastal patrols on board their yacht *Asgard* to land their cargo of 900 Mauser rifles and 25,000 rounds of ammunition in Howth at the end of July 1914.[2] The reception committee comprised 800 Volunteers, among them Arthur Griffith and Eamon de Valera. A few days later Conor O'Brien landed the balance of that consignment in Kilcoole, County Wicklow. Less publicised in this inflammatory gesture was the role of Sir Thomas Myles. Gogarty's former mentor in the Richmond Hospital put his seafaring experience to good effect when making a similar delivery on the Wicklow coast in his yacht *Chotah*.[3] That Sir Thomas could reconcile his actions with holding the position of Surgeon to the King in Ireland is indicative of the confusion and ambivalence that existed in Ireland at the time.

Sir Edward Grey's announcement of imminent war in August 1914 came to Winston Churchill as a curious relief from grappling with the Ulster Unionist problem, allowing the cabinet to turn aside from "the dreary steeples of Tyrone and Fermanagh". He and every relieved Loyalist seized upon this little fracas on the continent, fully expected to be "over by Christmas", as a welcome distraction. For his part, John Redmond, in return for the promise of Home Rule, now, understandably deferred in the face of German oppression, offered the services of his Volunteers. Gogarty was not among that number; at thirty-four he was almost too old to volunteer, even had he so wished. He was thus not among the droves of civil servants, merchants and professional men who enlisted out of an unthinking sense of duty and entrained to the Curragh Camp to be fashioned into – in all too many cases – cannon fodder. A quarter of a million Irishmen, and women, answered that call. And one in five paid the ultimate price.

CHAPTER TWENTY-FIVE

In the spring of 1915, not long after Joyce had embarked upon *Ulysses*, as it happened, Oliver St John Gogarty succumbed to what may well have been typhoid fever. Erroneously confused with typhus until the middle of the nineteenth century, typhoid fever is defined for mere laymen as "an infectious bacterial fever with an eruption of red spots on the chest and abdomen and severe intestinal irritation . . . the disease was formerly the scourge of armies, spread by contaminated water and by infection." The same source[1] discloses that Prince Albert died from typhoid fever in 1861, adding that more lives were lost in the Boer War from typhoid fever than from enemy action. If the Prince Consort could contract a fatal dose of typhoid fever in the rarified surroundings of the imperial court, then how much more susceptible was a practising physician doing his daily rounds in a public hospital?

Irrespective of how Gogarty contracted this potentially fatal disease, it was to the Meath Hospital that he was admitted for treatment, fortunately with happier results than the hapless poet James Clarence Mangan, who had ended his days there in 1849, aged only forty-six. As soon as the crisis had passed Gogarty wrote to his old friend and former inmate of the Martello Tower, James Starkie, by this time perhaps better known as Seumas O'Sullivan. "I am entering my third week – the Lethean week – of it now. Naturally I will meet death with dignity (not to mention diarrhoea)!!" As evidence of his improvement Gogarty included verses, entitled "Poets' Ward: From the Meath Hospital"[2]

A measure of just how debilitated Gogarty was left by this illness can be gained from his decision to convalesce by the coast. To this end he rented a villa in Sorrento Road, Dalkey, then called Seaview (latterly named Capri) for two full years. During that period he let 15 Ely Place and moved his consulting rooms to 32 St Stephen's Green, beside the Shelbourne Hotel. Over sixty years later Dublin Tourism erected a plaque to mark Gogarty's centenary. Among those present at the unveiling were his daughter Brenda and son Noll, who observed with wry amusement that the plaque had been placed not on the portion of the terrace where their father had practised, but on an adjacent one.

Quite to what extent Gogarty's illness and lengthy convalescence affected his income can only be conjectured. Likewise, the effects of Easter 1916 and its bloody aftermath must have disrupted his practice. Like Arthur Griffith, Gogarty had been kept unaware of plans for insurrection, which ran completely counter to the Irish Volunteers' maxim: "Defence, not defiance." He had been making his way back to Dublin from the west by train on Easter Monday when a delay in Athlone to facilitate the mobilisation of troops provided the first confirmation of the rumours of trouble in the capital. The train's progress was halted in Mullingar as the line had been cut. Gogarty hired a car to complete his journey, accompanied by local M.P. Larry Ginnell. Only when the windscreen was shattered by an insurgent's bullet as they travelled down Cabra Road did the reality of the uprising dawn on the intrepid motorists.

Recalling events many years later in his "unpremeditated autobiography", Gogarty claimed to have been broadly in sympathy with the sentiments and aspirations expressed in the notices posted up around the city proclaiming an Irish Republic.

"I got one of these proclamations and brought it home. It was printed on poor paper and there were at least two fonts of type used. It was badly punctuated: things which witnessed the secrecy and haste of its printing.

"I examined the names of the signatories first. Not one was known to me, except in one case and that was by reading of the exploits of James Connolly whose patriotism seemed to be the patriotism of a labour agitator. I had met not one of those who had proposed themselves as the Provisional Government."

Biographer J. B. Lyons has questioned the foregoing. "A statement difficult to credit today. Is one to attribute it to the faulty recall of a septuagenarian or has it the praiseworthy purpose of demythologising?"[3] Lyons had good reason to be sceptical, for it is hardly conceivable that Gogarty, through close association with Arthur Griffith and membership of the IRB, was unaware of Patrick Pearse. The principal of St Enda's school had been banned from a proposed meeting of the Gaelic Society in Trinity College in December 1914 by Vice-Provost Mahaffy, Gogarty's former mentor and subsequent friend. Similarly, Gogarty's involvement in the Irish literary movement of the day must have brought him in contact – however casual – with the poets Thomas MacDonagh, a protégé of W. B. Yeats, and Joseph Mary Plunkett. Although Gogarty's junior by almost a decade, Count Plunkett's tubercular son had likewise been educated at both Belvedere and Stoneyhurst before becoming a fellow-member of the IRB.

Gogarty's disavowal of the signatories of the proclamation appears ever more disingenuous in the light of his friendship with Sir Horace Plunkett, Edward Dunsany's uncle and founder of the co-operative movement in Ireland. As far back as 10 September 1897 Horace Plunkett had made the following entry in his diary: "to spend a morning at St. Enda's School and discuss the ideals of education with Pearse and MacDonagh, to catch a vivid minute with George Russell in Plunkett House, in the afternoon to see Yeats and Lady Gregory moving down the quays to rehearsal at the Abbey Theatre, and in the evening to hear a Synge play and pass a late hour with Kettle. An ambrosian night and day."

The following day Gogarty quizzed Hicks, the famous furniture maker in Lower Pembroke Street. "Tom Clarke is all right, an old Fenian. There's nothing wrong with Tom Clarke. Patrick Pearse? His father is a tombstone cutter over in England. Sean MacDiarmada has a bit of a limp. Eamon Ceannt is Edward Kent, born in England. Tom MacDonagh, I don't think he is a Dublin man. Joseph Plunkett? Isn't he one of the sons of auld Count Plunkett by one of his marriages, the old fellow with the beard? He had one son anyway who was riddled with tuberculosis . . . But what the Hell is all this to you?"

What indeed had it to do with anyone? The English artist Charles Ricketts hastened to assure a worried W. B. Yeats that no intelligent politician would fall into the trap of turning the leaders of an ill-conceived and generally unpopular insurrection into martyrs. Ricketts recorded his reassuring words in his diary. "A paternal government will discover Roger Casement was insane, imprison the leaders during the war pending investigations over the extent of German intrigues in the matter, discover that these men were misguided dupes, and probably amnesty them after the war."

Bemused by all the rumour and counter-rumour surrounding the course of the uprising, Gogarty decided that his first duty was the protection of his family. Patriotism, he thought, might manifest itself in kidnapping. Thus he returned, by divers means, to Connemara, where all was quiet.

"The newspapers came through. As I thought: the principals were held in prison in Dublin's infamous Kilmainham jail. There they awaited execution. General Maxwell was appointed to hold the city under military discipline. His idea of discipline was to shoot the rebels by twos. This will go down well in America where, in spite of all that is spent yearly in propaganda favourable to the British, the Irish have a voice."

Fifteen of the leaders were shot. De Valera could thank his American citizenship (he had been born in New York) for his reprieve, while Constance Markievicz was spared on account of her gender. Sir Roger Casement, apprehended in Kerry in his attempts to put off the Easter Rising, was hanged for treason, his name blackened and his trial hopelessly prejudiced by the prosecution's circulation of the infamous "black diaries". On re-reading his own diary, particularly his assurances to Yeats, Charles Ricketts merely added the rueful post-script, "I was an idiot."

That doleful series of executions had a remarkable effect on the mood of the Irish nation, very gradually transforming a bunch of misguided saboteurs, with nothing to lose but their lives, into martyrs for Ireland's freedom. In one view: "this rebellion has been the greatest mistake in Ireland's history and the method of its suppression the greatest error England has ever made in Ireland." That was an opinion. What was fact was the immediate and dramatic decline in enlistment, not just in

Ireland, but conspicuously in Australia. Another fact that emerged was the preponderance of Christian Brothers' pupils who had turned out on Easter Monday. While the Brothers' schools in Marino, Synge Street and Westland Row had educated eighty-four of the insurgents, a massive one hundred and twenty-five – including Sean Heuston, Con Colbert and Eamonn Ceannt – had attended the O'Connell School in North Richmond Street. The Christian Brothers Schools were noted for turning out young men with a highly developed sense of national identity and a particular pride in being Irish. By contrast, just four of those apprehended in the aftermath of Easter Monday had been educated by the Jesuits in nearby Belvedere. That Gogarty should have extolled the merits of the Christian Brothers over the Jesuits, while Joyce held a diametrically opposed view of the two teaching orders, remained one of the anomalies of their relationship.

Gogarty duly contributed his sonnet "The Rebels"[4] to *Aftermath of Easter Week*, which appeared anonymously the following year, to raise money for the dependents of those who had paid the supreme penalty and in doing so ignited a semi-national resolve to be rid of the British yoke.

Gogarty's recollections of the Easter Rising and its aftermath evoke the words of F. W. Maitland: "What now lies in the past once lay in the future." For whatever reason, Gogarty made no reference to the following, curious reaction on his part to those momentous events. One of the few surviving letters from his brother Henry,[5] written from the Law Department, Southern Pacific Company, San Francisco, 20 November 1916, is the key.

"Dear Oliver, As to selling your picture by William Orpen out here in the West, I am afraid that it would be impossible for several reasons . . . prosperity still hasn't spread to the West coast . . . the 1915 Exhibition did well in the sale of pictures and people are pretty well loaded up . . . get Burke's advice as to the proper person in New York. Henry Clay Frick the New York millionaire is a great collector of pictures. He would probably direct some agent in London of Duveen Brothers to view the picture and price it for him."

Henry wrote briefly of other matters, before alluding to his hunting friends from days of yore in Tipperary, "Burke is leaving Grove and auctioning off all his furniture, pictures, etc. Your fond brother, Henry H. Gogarty." Apart from the formality of his signature, the reference to the Burkes leaving Grove implies that, at least as far as Henry is aware, his older brother had completely lost touch with their erstwhile family friends down the country in Fethard. The disposal of Grove marked the end of an era in the opinion of an anonymous hunting historian.

"The succession of short Masterships, coupled with the disturbing days of the Land League, left Tipperary hunt in a sorry state, from which they were rescued in 1887 by Richard Burke – the beginning of the most famous Mastership in the history of the Tipperary hunt. Few men ever did more in the cause of fox-hunting than Richard Burke. Described as one of the most dauntless men to hounds in Ireland, he showed great sport, and among his many historical hunts, that which took place from Meldrum in 1888 was the most outstanding, the point being eight miles and the distance 18 as hounds ran. During his Mastership, Mr. Burke built kennels and stables at Grove, the cradle of the Tipperary hunt."[6]

It could also be that Henry was trying to establish common ground with his brother in that letter, for the mode of signature would suggest that they were on less than intimate terms. Alternatively, that harking back to times past could have reflected the fact that Oliver was the only member of the immediate family left in Ireland. Mayflo had remained abroad, while Richard, the youngest, having worked for the Argyll Motor Company in Dublin, had recently emigrated. "The only one [of the three sons] who was not given a profession or sent to an University. He left Dublin about forty years ago in a red shirt to seek his fortune in the Argentine." So Gogarty would write to his son Noll in 1953.

Gogarty's attempt to find an American buyer for his portrait by Orpen may have been motivated by reasons other than financial necessity. Indeed, his actions the following year tend to discount money as a motive. Orpen had moved to London, to take advantage of an infinitely larger and more affluent clientele, becoming well established at the outbreak of war in August 1914. He shared the general belief that the war would be over by Christmas. Indeed, over the next twelve months his income from portraits alone amounted to £7,700, indicative of how remote the ongoing struggle in the trenches had remained from him. Then conscription was introduced in December 1915. Deaf to Sean Keating's entreaties to return with him to Ireland, Orpen enlisted, declaring: "Everything I have I owe to England." The events of Easter 1916 ended any ambivalence among those who had kept a foot in either camp. And Orpen had declared for England.

A friend of far longer, and closer standing, Tom Kettle, had also volunteered, utterly dismayed and disillusioned by the events of Easter 1916. As a proponent of constitutional reform and negotiated self-determination for Ireland, he had been horrified by that cock-eyed attempt at armed insurrection and the savage, senseless assassinations that ensued. His alienation could be measured in terms of an earlier retort of his to an observation that Dublin Castle did not understand Ireland. "Did it not know what the Irish people want, it could not so infallibly have maintained its tradition of giving them the opposite." The murder, by a deranged British officer, of the pacifist Francis Sheehy-Skeffington, who had co-edited the *Nationalist* with him, decided Kettle's course of action – join the struggle for the freedom of small nations. He left for the front in July and met his death at Ginchy on 9 September. In a letter to his wife, Mary, from the front Tom Kettle vowed that, if spared, he would take her to live somewhere down the country and there cultivate early potatoes. And that is a matter of record. Unrecorded was his farewell to Neenie Gogarty, who bade him Godspeed and looked forward to his safe return. He looked her in the eye and told her calmly, almost apologetically, that for him there would be no homecoming. A sonnet written to his daughter Betty days before his death contained what was to become his epitaph.

> *So here, while the mad guns curse overhead,*
> *And tired men sigh with mud for couch and floor,*
> *Know that we fools, now with the foolish dead,*
> *Died not for flag, nor King nor Emperor,*
> *But for a dream, born in a herdsman's shed,*
> *And for the secret Scripture of the poor.*

Tom Kettle was one of only three men of whom Gogarty would neither utter nor entertain any derogatory comment, however witty, however warranted. He wrote of his school friend's death: "He died as it befitted his breed, in battle, and he spent a great soul. When the news came of Tom Kettle's death, there were eyelashes, and not only women's, that were wet with tears."

In more reflective vein Gogarty appraised his late friend and ideal among men: "his spirits which were constantly high, his wit that was as good-natured as himself, and his attitude to life that is a revelation to those who cannot but think of it as being as humdrum as themselves. There is a different land from this and a life to be lived therein, and it took Tom Kettle to reveal it to us with all his blithe strength."

Such was Gogarty's estimation of his dead friend; nothing short of a memorial, erected on a prominent site in Dublin, would suffice, he declared. Getting wind of this proposal, Stephen Gwynn wrote to Gogarty saying that Lady Scott had offered to help to the extent that only the cost of materials and erection remained to be found. Kathleen Scott, widowed when her husband, the Antarctic explorer Robert Falcon Scott perished in his losing race to the South Pole against the Norwegian Amundsen in 1912, was an established sculptress, whose statue of her late husband was erected in Waterloo Place, London. In due course Gogarty's plan came to fruition, when Albert Power's bronze bust of Tom Kettle was erected on the perimeter of St Stephen's Green, facing the College of Surgeons.

Therein lies another Irish anomaly that causes incomprehension amongst outsiders and a shrug of resignation from those closer to home. Tom Kettle, killed in World War One in the service of the British Army, was commemorated by a bust in Dublin's most prominent park. Yet, the 200,000 Irish men and women who fought the same fight for the same cause and lived to return to their native land found themselves shunned and derided as traitors to auld Ireland, unemployable outside the Pale – pariahs. Even as late as 1966, at the fiftieth anniversary of the Easter Rising, a mean-minded Irish government refused to recognise the valour and the value of the 250,000 Irish who had risked their lives for the freedom of small nations, not least their own.

Safely ensconced by this time in Zurich, and thus protected by Swiss neutrality, while the rest of Europe became progressively engulfed in war, James Joyce had come to regard 1916 as a singularly lucky year for him. Through the combined intercession of W. B. Yeats, Ezra Pound and Lady Cunard he had secured a Civil List pension from the British government of £100 a year, ordained by Prime Minister Asquith. Better still, the tireless efforts of Harriet Weaver had at last yielded a publisher for *A Portrait of the Artist as a Young Man* – the New York firm of B. W. Huebsch. So convinced had Joyce become of the efficacy of 1916, he persuaded his publisher to use that year in the imprint, whether or not it was strictly accurate. By contrast, Stannie can have found little to savour about 1916. Having refused to heed the signs of unrest in Italy and seek the sanctuary of Switzerland, Stannie had been interned in Austria, and there remained for the duration of the war.

CHAPTER TWENTY-SIX

'I am looking for the largest house, farthest from the railhead in Ireland, something that may be even two days away, because this afternoon I saw an automobile that will bring that house within half a day's reach in allowing for the lag in human thinking. I want to get it while it is still unsaleable, while it is still cheap.'

Renvyle House, "in the heart of Connemara on the edge of the sea on the last shelf of Europe in the next parish to New York," filled Gogarty's demands. He bought it, "out of the proceeds of my teetotalism", as he wrote to Dermot Freyer. Seized from the O'Flaherty's in the aftermath of the Cromwellian conquest of Ireland, Renvyle estate had been acquired in 1680 by Henry Blake, a member of one of the fourteen "tribes" of Galway city. In the early part of the nineteenth century a descendant and namesake had taken possession of the estate from the O'Flahertys, who had acted as middlemen in the interim, built himself a large, spacious, sturdy, weather-slated house and lived there with his family. While there they wrote *Letters from the Irish Highlands*, published in London in 1825. Caroline Blake, the last of that name to inhabit Renvyle House, had opened her home as an hotel as early as 1883, soldiering on there despite constant hostility from the militant Land League movement. For Gogarty, the purchase of Renvyle, that "long, long house in the ultimate land of the undiscovered West", was a tangible realisation of his love affair with Connemara, which had grown and grown since his very first visit to his in-laws in Garranbaun, just a few miles south as the crow flies on the other side of Ballinakill Bay.

Yet again the gods seemed to have smiled on Gogarty, who only bought Renvyle because he had no inkling that his sister-in-law was obliged to dispose of Garranbaun. Bernard Duane, Gogarty's father-in-law, had died in 1913, followed by his wife Barbara three years later. Neenie's undated letter to him from Renvyle shortly after its purchase confirms the situation. "The house I found in good order but the grass outside, gardens and drive are nearly as neglected as when I got the place . . . I am sending for the furniture to Garranbaun. It is reported that we are going to sell this place and buy Garranbaun – otherwise Mrs Bailey (née Twining) would bid for Garranbaun. She is very wealthy – if she did it might solve all the difficulties." Later in the same letter she exhorted her husband to send the governess down to assist her: "train from Broadstone leaves 1.30 – Clifden 8.00pm."[1]

Blanche Bailey was the youngest of five daughters of Frederick Twining, an engineer and member of the famous London tea company. Frederick's family had purchased nine hundred acres around Cleggan, once a thriving fishing port nearby, on the dispersal of the Martyn estate – then the largest in these islands – in the aftermath of the famine of 1845. Blanche married William W. Bailey, a pioneering rubber planter in Malaya. They had enjoyed considerable success on the Turf and established a stud farm in County Limerick. Widowed in 1910, Blanche Bailey continued to run the stud in Limerick, eventually retiring to Cleggan where she ended her days.[2]

Garranbaun became the property of a syndicate; common practice with sporting properties in the West of Ireland in days when fish and game were still abundant. Sadly, the tradition that attached to Garranbaun, whereby its owners experienced all manner of misfortunes, was destined to continue. While Gogarty may have initially regretted missing out on an opportunity to purchase his in-laws' property, they may indeed have done him a favour. Local legend has long maintained that the ghost of a "military man", who came to a gruesome end, haunts the driveway in front of this beautifully sited Georgian-style house built in the 1850s. From the front windows of Garranbaun, looking inland across Ballinakill Bay to the Twelve Bens, Rossdhu, home of Neenie's brother Mathias, could be seen. It was against that backdrop that Gogarty had had his wife and three young children painted in 1916 by Gerald Brockhurst.

Gerald Brockhurst, born in Birmingham, had crossed to Ireland, having been rejected for military service when conscription had been introduced in Britain. His arrival was timely, in that he replaced Orpen in Gogarty's eclectic array of painter friends, headed then by Augustus John. In *It Isn't This Time of Year at All!* Gogarty gave Brockhurst the name "Snodgrass".

"I was intent on having the children painted, and so they were. The painting, sadly mutilated by the louts whom an alien loosed on the country when he plunged it into civil war, still exists, patched up by some expert in Chelsea. So do three magnificent water colours of the children."

Ironically, Gogarty's rapturous infatuation with Connemara and its ever-changing skies was not shared by Neenie. As can so often be the case, Neenie had embraced her nursing career in Dublin and then espoused her husband by way of escape from the social wasteland that Connemara was to her. She had seen all too many fall prey to the superficial charms of that beautiful but essentially barren region. After all, any of her own family who had made anything of themselves had done so by getting out of Connemara. Mat, her brother, had sailed to the Argentine to seek his fortune. For all her Victorian gentility and refinement Neenie quickly realised the dangers inherent in allowing her husband give rein to his dangerously impractical and romantic nature in an environment in which, as her son Noll would later observe, "The Duanes had been going broke for over a thousand years!"[3]

Evidence of Neenie's misgivings has survived in her letters from Connemara to her husband, busily doctoring in Dublin. In them she compared and contrasted the stifling, claustrophobic ambience of Heather Island, which Gogarty had purchased in tandem with Renvyle House, with the wide open, breezy spaces of Portmarnock. Neenie was not the first woman to visualise marriage as an escape from her own family and surroundings – and certainly not the last. Feminine intuition warned her that Oliver's infatuation with what she regarded as the siren summons of Connemara would prove their downfall. Towards the end of her life – homeless following the loss of Renvyle House – Neenie blamed her destitution squarely on her husband's love affair with Connemara. "When I think of all that I once had – and now am left with nothing."[4]

CHAPTER TWENTY-SEVEN

As Gogarty enjoyed his Golden Age in Connemara, while continuing his practice in Dublin, James Joyce had at last begun to perceive some glimmer of light at what had proved a very, very long tunnel in his struggles to become established. *A Portrait of the Artist as a Young Man* was published in New York in December 1916 and in London two months later. The mixture of critical acclaim and satisfactory sales moved Joyce to write to Ezra Pound in July 1917 concerning his real preoccupation.[1]

Now let awhile my messmates be
My ponderous Penelope
And my Ulysses born anew
In Dublin as an Irish Jew.
With them I'll sit, with them I'll drink
Nor heed what press and pressmen think
Nor leave their rockbound house of joy
For Helen or for windy Troy.

One who did not join in the critical acclaim of Joyce's book was Joseph Holloway, Dublin theatre buff and recorder. He conveyed his views in his diary for 22 September 1917. "I finished reading James Joyce's crudely compiled book, *A Portrait of the Artist as a Young Man*, in which he succeeds in introducing more coarseness of language and filthy expressions than any book I ever came across."

A month later Holloway's diary contains this plaintive entry. "William Butler Yeats, the poet, was wed in London to Miss Georgi[n]a Hyde-Lees, the only daughter of the late Mr. W. G. Hyde-Lees of Pickhill Hall, Wrexham, and of Mrs. Henry Tucker, 16 Montpelier Square, London. The wedding was a quiet affair. He was born 52 years ago, and was only 24 when his literary talent began to blossom. What will poor Lady Gregory do now?" Early in December Holloway's diary reveals in more detail the grounds for his concern that Yeats' marriage might diminish the quality of life in the capital.

"Here in Dublin were it not for the little Abbey Theatre and its interesting plays and players, we would have nothing to go to in the way of plays. Our theatres have fallen into the hands of showmen, who have turned them into music-halls or worse in their craving to make money, till at last they have succeeded in killing all taste for the theatre in the old play-going class, and even the people they attracted to the fifth-rate variety stuff they provided have got tired of such-like rubbish, and are rapidly deserting such-like performances for the Pictures, where they can see lurid melodramas, set in beautiful surroundings, capably enacted on the screen, to music from a more or less orchestral accompaniment.

"I was at the Abbey last night where an amusing comedy, *Fox and Geese*, was revived with success, with *In the Shadow of the Glen* as a first piece. The Abbey Company under Fred O'Donovan is becoming quite a good repertory company of very capable players . . . Next week we are promised a new slum play by Dr. Oliver Gogarty, which may, by all accounts, create talk and controversy."

In the intervening period W. B. Yeats had spent part of his honeymoon with his bride as guests of the Gogartys in Renvyle House. "George", almost thirty years younger than her husband, was a medium. It was their mutual interest in the occult that had drawn them together in the twilight of Yeats' many thwarted infatuations, grounds for Joyce's scorn in his "Holy Office". Her psychic powers were soon called into play to determine the cause behind certain most disturbing phenomena, which particularly affected the Gogarty children, aged between six and ten. To her credit, Georgie reached a more or less tolerable accommodation with the spirit of a young, mentally deranged Blake boy, who confessed to her his disquiet at strangers occupying his ancestral home.

Various people have recorded their accounts of what took place on that occasion in Renvyle House, though perhaps none so entertainingly as Seymour Leslie in *The Jerome Connexion.*

"W. B. Yeats sat reciting his latest poems, surrounded by the Gogarty family in the long low library of the old Blake manor house, panelled from shipwrecks. The peaty fire gave off a pungent odour as the backdraught from the Atlantic gale blew the blue smoke out to envelope us with its incense.

"Oliver St. John Gogarty, retired surgeon of Dublin, Greek scholar, wit, poet, the best talker in Ireland, a character in *Ulysses* which Joyce indeed opens in the Martello Tower that Gogarty had leased. With Yeats, George Moore and 'AE', he was of that select company pinned down for ever in Moore's *Hail and Farewell.* But his wit had a malicious edge to it, and he had made many personal enemies in a country where personal relations are supreme. His practical jokes had not endeared him, he had in particular declared his aversion to de Valera thus taking up a position in the impending civil war; in the event he was to fly for his life by swimming amid the swans of the Liffey and then to lose his home which had been fired in his absence. He had written some charming poems, many of them bawdy, and two plays.

"Yeats continued to read on in a sing-song voice that nearly put us to sleep, when the door in front of us, next to the chimney, slowly unlatched, and opened wide – to reveal an empty passage: the house was notorious for its hauntings. We all started up but Yeats, with a magisterial wave of his beautiful hand, and without otherwise interrupting the flow of his song, said, 'Leave It alone – It will go away as it came.' The obedient door closed. For Yeats was not a mere medium, he was that rare being, Master of spirits, a Controller. It was not the first time I had met him and marvelled at such physical distinction . . .

"Whether it was the mastery of Yeats or the medium qualities of his wife, a Cornishwoman of psychic powers, the atmosphere in the house-party next day was increasingly disturbed by manifestations. Evan Morgan had arrived and was thrilled to learn of the room haunted by the Renvyle ghost, said to be that of an idiot son they had locked up in it. Gogarty said it was now empty – indeed no furniture could be left there as a heavy wardrobe had been moved by something across the door so they had to break in through the window . . .

"Evan had just been received into the Church of Rome: 'by good fortune I have with me a potent reliquary, come with me and I will exorcise the poor ghost.' I had increasing doubts of his authority as a layman to do any such thing but was unprepared for the dramatic consequence as he lit three candles 'for the Trinity – and harmony' and uttered some Latin prayers. The results were not what he expected.

"For the room immediately filled with a thick mist and in no time Evan was thrown to the floor, groaning, his fists clenched in his eyes, 'for God's sake, get me out of here.' I dragged him out, called for Gogarty and together we placed him on his bed. 'Suffering from shock' said the doctor and immediately applied remedies. Evan confessed as he came to, 'I went down into the private hell of that poor boy! I've never known such mental agony! Hand me my Catullus, I won't come down to dinner.'

"Yeats took the news with a calm indifference, making no comment, and Gogarty was to write a chapter on the incident in his famous *As I was Going Down Sackville Street*. Characteristically he tells it all wrong and even makes Yeats, who certainly was holding a séance with his wife and the Gogartys at the moment Evan began his 'exorcising', remark that I was a 'vortex of spirits'; a nickname that was to pursue me."[2]

The play to which Holloway looked forward with such relish had, incredibly, only been submitted – incomplete – for Lady Gregory's evaluation in early November, with a covering letter from Gogarty. "A friend of mine has a Dublin play nearly ready. I have had a hand in it. It is of the slums and public boards and likely to cause a stir. If it is to take on it should be on the stage by Xmas. If the Abbey refuse it the Irishwomen's reform league may take the Gaiety for it. I want the Abbey to have it if you think it good enough. May I send you two Acts to read?"

Despite the daunting lack of rehearsal time, Lady Gregory agreed to stage the play, which she found "very stirring." Her prediction was to prove accurate. "I think it will be a great success and will do real good in stirring up public indignation. Some may fall on us, but we shall suffer in a good cause." Fred O'Donovan, besides producing *Blight*, also took the lead role as the roguish Stanislaus Tully. Others who took part and later went on to theatrical renown included Michael MacLiammoir, Maureen Delaney, Barry Fitzgerald and Arthur Shields.

Joseph Holloway's eager anticipation and assessment of the much-touted Gogarty play prompted a diary entry that same night, Tuesday, 11 December 1917.

"Not for years has such an audience been inside the Abbey as assembled tonight to see the first performance of *Blight*, a play of Dublin slum life by A. and O. (Dr. Oliver Gogarty and Joseph O'Connor, Heblon of *Studies in Blue* fame). To me the audience was quite as interesting as the play. In the vestibule before eight were grouped together Con Curran, Conroy (the Gaelic writer), Susan Mitchell and her sister, George Russell, Mr. and Mrs. Darrell Figgis, Mrs. Stopford Green, Seumas O'Sullivan, Estelle Solomons, Lady Gregory, Mr. and Mrs. James Stephens, George Roberts and Mrs. (*née* Maire Garvey), and crowds of other well-known figures . . .

"The theatre was abuzz with excitement before the play began; it had got about that the play might be suppressed after the first performance – that, in fact, it was very 'hot stuff'. So all rushed to be there; just as the Royal was crowded before twelve o'clock on Saturday morning to witness *Ghosts* in the hope of being shocked. In both cases those who went with that intention must have been sadly disappointed. *Ghosts* merely proved very dull as a stage play, and *Blight* quite interesting to Dubliners, as it discussed a problem sincerely that eats into the very heart of our city, and treats it with a certain amount of crude realism . . . but, nevertheless, brought home its lesson – that the evils of the slums can never be checked by charity nor extension of hospitals, but at its own roots alone. Check the evil that creates slums, and slums vanish and all the evils they create. Such is the lesson to be learned in witnessing *Blight*, a tragedy of Dublin.

"On meeting Conroy in the vestibule on coming out, he summed up what he had seen as, 'A discussion with interruptions.' 'From the audience?' I queried.

"'No, from the characters,' he replied . . . The general opinion was that the piece was more a discussion than a play, and that the characters argued rather than conversed."

Holloway's "A and O" was his shorthand for "Alpha" and "Omega", the first and final letters of the Greek alphabet, further symbolising the start and finish of the human experience. These pseudonyms served as a threadbare disguise for Gogarty and Joseph O'Connor. The latter, who provided timely and indeed vital assistance with dialogue revisions, had impressed Gogarty with his series of articles on slum life published in the *Evening Mail*. Joseph O'Connor went on to become a judge, outliving his collaborator long enough to contribute to his kinsman's biography of Gogarty.

Those who could not get tickets for the first night and appreciated good theatre as opposed to witnessing a *cause célèbre* were duly reassured by reviews in their morning newspapers, notably the *Irish Independent*.

"Such an audience has not been at the Abbey since the night Shaw's *Blanco Posnet* was first produced [banned by the Lord Chamberlain in England and first staged in Ireland]. *Blight* is the tragedy of Dublin – the horrible, terrible, creeping crawling spectre that haunts the slumdom of the capital of Ireland. It is not horror for horror's sake. That charge may not be levelled at the authors with any hope that it can be maintained, for if I understand aright the meaning of the painters of this lurid picture it is this: Slumdom is the nest of vice; charity as a palliative is no cure. The Charity in fact that endows hospitals and helps those institutions to extend their premises and cater for increased cases is misdirected Charity. Away with the seat of disease!"

The controversy surrounding *Blight* arose in the main from its being based quite blatantly on the Housing Inquiry of 1914, which had pinpointed obvious conflict of interests on the part of fourteen members of Dublin Corporation. It transpired that all of them were owners of tenement properties or small cottages. Indeed, three of them owned a total of sixty-one slum properties. Worse still, C. H. O'Connor, President of the Inquiry, had found, on personal inspection, that properties belonging to Alderman Corrigan, Councillor Crozier and Alderman O'Reilly were officially classified as being unfit for human habitation. While Gogarty had already demonstrated an appetite for controversy, Lady Gregory and her fellow directors of the Abbey ran a considerable risk in putting on such an accusatory play.

Blight continued to fill the Abbey for the week in which it ran, yielding box-office receipts of £190 – a record. After a further three nights at the beginning of January the play was taken off, for fear, it was rumoured, of reprisals from official quarters, which the Abbey's parlous resources could ill-afford. For their part the co-authors received £10. Gogarty immediately sent his portion to what was known as the Herald Boot Fund; his way of publicising Lady Gregory's renowned parsimony towards playwrights.

This minimal gesture of defiance was as close as Gogarty would ever come to casting aspersions on Lady Gregory, at least while that formidable woman still lived. Not, indeed, that he was alone in being in awe of the black-swathed chatelaine of Coole Park. Even the lofty Yeats, who could do nothing wrong in Lady Gregory's eyes, admitted that, on visiting Coole Park as a mature and famous married man, he lost his nerve in the face of his hostess's aversion to animals in the house. Rather than confront his hostess with his pet cat, Pangur, he had the animal secreted in the stables until the household had retired for the night. Only then did he creep out to the stables and retrieve his abandoned feline. Frank O'Connor, narrator of that tale, held that "The old lady was a holy terror; that is the only way I can describe her . . . Of all the women I knew she had the most powerful will . . . She always knew precisely what she wanted and set about getting it." Lennox Robinson, her long-suffering manager of the Abbey for many years, left a delightful example of the old lady's doughtiness. In the midst of an ambush in O'Connell Street, when all the passers-by were prone on the pavement under a hail of English machine-guns, one diminutive old lady in her widow's weeds stood defiantly erect shouting "Up de rebels!"[3]

The authors of *John Stanislaus Joyce*[4] would subsequently view *Blight* from a predictably different perspective. "As an Abbey controversy it ranked between Shaw's *Blanco Posnet* and the imminent dramas of Sean O'Casey." However, it did not escape their vigilance that, although *Blight* was unquestionably a serious piece, "James's old rival had used it to ridicule the Joyces. It featured characters such as a labourer called Stanislaus and a crippled son called Jimmy, and contains a knowing or mocking reprise of elements taken from the home life of the Joyces as it was known to Gogarty. Oliver Gogarty had once at least had to go to John Stanilaus's house, when Eva had refused to walk through Dublin carrying the man's suit that Gogarty was lending to James. *Blight* also featured as light relief 'Medical Dick' and 'Medical Davy', comic turns from the college banter between Jim and Gogarty that Joyce would use in *Ulysses*. It is highly likely that the Joyces recognised themselves here, for a little time after the play opened in early 1918 Charlie Joyce wrote the author a letter: 'Dear Mr Gogarty, Can you lend me £1 . . .' They had been awkward drinking pals back in 1904. Perhaps Charlie was showing his true Joyce colours by claiming royalties . . . Neither Jim nor his stately ex-friend, now engaged with Arthur Griffith and Michael Collins in the creation of a new Ireland, would have been much amused by Charlie's appeal."

Gogarty had achieved his specific objective in *Blight*, creating public debate on the appalling housing conditions, in which the poor of Dublin existed, contracted disease and died. He had had a point to make, to which theatre had lent dramatic emphasis in a way that speeches and addresses had not. The writing of plays was not to him an end in itself. Unbeknownst to Gogarty, or to anybody else, one young man who saw *Blight* was sufficiently inspired by what he witnessed to become one of the greatest Irish playwrights. John Casey had lost his father when he was only twelve and was at this time nursing his dying mother in Dickensian squalor such as Gogarty depicted in *Blight*.

Already involved in the IRB and then in the ITGWU, Casey had become disenchanted with James Connolly's "sell-out" of the union movement to Pearce's doomed uprising in Easter 1916. Inspired by *Blight*, Sean O Cathasaigh – as he styled himself until the Abbey simplified it to Sean O'Casey – wrote his famous trilogy, which became the Abbey's economic lifeline for decades. *Juno and the Paycock*, staged for the first time on 3 March 1924, is similar in many respects to *Blight*. O'Casey freely acknowledged the influence and inspiration, while describing Gogarty as "a man who is greater than he will permit himself to be."

CHAPTER TWENTY-EIGHT

Nervousness on the part of the management of the Abbey about the authorities' possible reaction to *Blight* – ostensibly a play about the Dublin slums – becomes easier to appreciate in the light of political upheaval both at home and abroad in 1917. In March the first Russian revolution had resulted in the overthrow of the Tsar and the formation of a Provisional Government. In November a second Russian convulsion saw the Bolsheviks seize control. Closer to home the United States entered the European conflict in April and Eamon de Valera, an American citizen, was released from an English jail, along with Constance Markievicz, Joseph McGuinness and Eoin McNeill, following their part in the Easter Rising. Their compatriots, interned without trial, had been released in December 1916. In the general election Sinn Fein obliterated the old Irish Parliamentary party, but refused to take their seats in Westminster. In July the doomed Irish Convention opened in Dublin, under the chairmanship of Sir Horace Plunkett, in a futile attempt to resolve the knotty problem of Ulster's status in the event of Ireland being granted a measure of self-determination under the Home Rule Bill. Three months later Thomas Ashe, a republican prisoner, died in Mountjoy jail as a result of being forcibly fed while on hunger strike. In October Eamon de Valera, MP for County Clare, took over as President of Sinn Fein following Arthur Griffith's decision to stand down in the face of increasingly militant factions. And all the while the wanton, futile slaughter in the trenches continued.

Matters got if anything worse the following year. In April 1918 the Irish Conscription Act became law. It was unanimously rejected by all shades of political and religious opinions and factions throughout the island.

While the Act was never in fact implemented, it had the effect of uniting hitherto disparate political parties to a degree to which no indigenous appeal could ever have aspired.

Amidst all this political turmoil and increasing revulsion at the atrocities of the war in Europe, the cultural renaissance somehow carried on unabated in Ireland, which, as all Dubliners well knew, effectively meant the capital. Gogarty, who had published *Hyperthuleana*, his first book of verse, for private circulation, two years earlier, followed up now with a major contribution to *Secret Springs of Dublin Song*. Published both in Dublin by the Talbot Press and in London by Fisher Unwin, this anthology, with a Preface by Susan Mitchell, contained poems by numerous others including Lord Dunsany and Seumas O'Sullivan. One of Gogarty's fifteen unsigned submissions – "On the Death of His Aunt"[1] – was destined to give rise to lasting confusion. It was sub-titled: "To the Gravediggers to inter her gently."

Once again the tide of events put art and literature in Ireland on the back boiler. In May Arthur Griffith, for all his pacifist utterances, was arrested in the so-called "German Plot" along with over eighty other prominent republicans, among them de Valera and W. T. Cosgrave. Two months later Sinn Fein, the Irish Volunteers and the Gaelic League were proscribed. A fortnight later came news of the execution of Tsar Nicholas of Russia and his entire family. In October over five hundred perished when the m. v. *Leinster* was sunk by a German torpedo en route from Kingstown to Holyhead. At long, long last, at the eleventh hour of the eleventh day of the eleventh month of 1918, Armistice was declared. "What now lies in the past once lay in the future"; according to one reputable source, "Overall military fatalities in the First World War are generally put at about 9.8 million men, but some estimates exceed 12 million, and different figures for numbers of wounded start at around 20 million."[2] Of the estimated 250,000 Irishmen and women who took part, 50,000 paid the ultimate price in what became known as "the war to end all wars".

CHAPTER TWENTY-NINE

By one of those ghastly ironies that we can acknowledge but never explain the appalling carnage and waste of life that came to its futile conclusion on 11 November 1918 overlapped latterly with the influenza pandemic known as "Spanish flu". This viral infection spread across Europe and the Middle East in the autumn of 1918. By the middle of October the virus was killing over 1,200 each day in Paris alone. Deaths in Britain attributable to "Spanish flu" exceeded 200,000. On the other side of the Atlantic it claimed over 400,000 lives in the United States, the bulk of the casualties being otherwise perfectly healthy people between the ages of twenty and forty.

Gogarty was among thousands afflicted in Ireland, opting to convalesce in Renvyle House in March 1919. As ever, his recuperation was expedited by news of colourful company. Lady Leslie had accepted an invitation to celebrate Easter as the Gogartys' guest in Renvyle. Leonie Leslie was one of the celebrated Jerome sisters from New York, heiresses famed for their beauty. One sister, Jennie, married Lord Randolph Churchill, giving birth to Winston Churchill, then in the political wilderness following the slaughter of the Expeditionary Forces at Gallipoli. The other, Clara, married the adventurer Moreton Frewen. Her daughter, Clare Sheridan, became an accomplished, if controversial sculptress. While Gogarty was destined to cross swords with Winston Churchill on their first encounter following the Treaty,[1] he would remain friendly with Shane Leslie, Leonie's son, throughout his life.

Arthur Griffith, Gogarty's closest contact in the gathering movement for Irish self-determination, was incarcerated in an English prison on 21 January 1919 when the 3rd Brigade of the Irish Republican Army shot and killed two members of the Royal Irish Constabulary at Soloheadbeg in County Tipperary. That inglorious action was later defined as the commencement of the War of Independence. From his prison cell Griffith predicted that this kind of outlaw behaviour would, inexorably, lead to Irishmen killing Irishmen. On his release in March, Griffith returned to Dublin, assuming the post of Home Minister in the proscribed Dáil Éireann. While he was to become acting-President during de Valera's prolonged absence in the United States, Griffith acknowledged that the hawks had wrested the mantle from the doves. Although in many respects unlikely companions, Griffith and Gogarty were as one in their abhorrence of violence for political ends. W. T. Cosgrave was another of their persuasion, whereas de Valera, Michael Collins and his inseparable accomplice Harry Boland were committed proponents of armed combat and guerrilla warfare.

Just as he had when attacking the corrupt system of local government that underpinned the continuing scandal of the Dublin slums in *Blight*, Gogarty resorted to the stage and satire. *A Serious Thing* was staged for the first time in the Abbey on 19 August 1919. A one-act farce attributed to one "Gideon Ouseley", *A Serious Thing* concerns a Roman soldier guarding the tomb of Lazarus in Judea during Pontius Pilate's administration. He is joined by a centurion and another soldier, a Jewish conscript. Significantly, all the soldiers were dressed in khaki, "well known and widely distributed", as the programme notes wryly observed. The British officers in the audience found the skit hilarious, taking it at face value. Others were quick to perceive that the Romans represented British imperial oppression, with Lazarus the symbol of the failed Easter Rising. Joseph Holloway conceded that "the moment the dead Lazarus awoke from his tomb to join those who wished their country free was the cream of a very [brutal?] joke." Another reviewer used the contrast with Padraic Colum's *The Fiddler's House*, which preceded it, to write: "The only irresistibly funny episode of the night was 'A Serious Thing' – a farcical play by a gentleman who conceals his identity under the title of Gideon Ouseley. It is very brief, and simply kept the house in shrieks of laughter in which they indulged with all the greater gusto perhaps because of the melancholy experiences of the early part of the night."[2]

Gogarty was to use the same pseudonym for *The Enchanted Trousers*, his third and final play to be staged, as well as for his autobiographical novel *Tumbling in the Hay*. The real Gideon Ouseley (1762-1839) was one of the Ouseleys of Dunmore, County Galway. Having converted to the Methodist faith in 1791, Gideon Ouseley became a forceful and courageous preacher, unafraid to deliver rousing sermons in Irish to native audiences, regardless of the personal risks that such "heretical' mob oratory incurred. In a letter to Horace Reynolds many years later[3] Gogarty credited his friend, John Elwood, with the discovery of Ouseley's polemics in the National Library of Ireland as a source of comic references.

The Joyce family apparently found no grounds to take offence at *A Serious Thing*. And those who now habitually perused Gogarty's writings for slights, real or imagined, discerned instead mild jibes at the particular expense of his wealthy friend and Connemara neighbour, the eccentric explorer Talbot Clifton, some of whose expressions Gogarty put in the mouth of the centurion, notably "Looky here now!" The more diligent were insistent that the various references to the occult and spirit-rapping were directed at W. B. Yeats and his wife George.[4]

Fired by the success of his two plays so far staged in the Abbey, Gogarty promptly followed up with *The Enchanted Trousers*. Another one-act satire, *The Enchanted Trousers* poked fun at Sir Horace Plunkett's "Department" by which its founder sought to reform Irish agriculture, albeit with a completely English staff. With only a week to go before its first night, revisions were causing problems in rehearsal, as Joseph Holloway recorded.

"Peter Nolan came up after rehearsing *The Enchanted Trousers* at the Abbey, and told me that Dr. Gogarty was always changing the text, so much so that they gave him only until tomorrow to continue doing so, as they never could learn and unlearn the various texts by Tuesday next . . . Yeats has ceased to take any interest in the theatre. Robinson now does take an added interest. It is shyness that makes Robinson so aloof and awkward in his manner, Nolan says."

In the event Holloway seemed ambivalent as to whether everything did indeed come right on the night. "I . . . went to the Abbey for the first night of *The Enchanted Trousers*, a play (or satire) in one act by Gideon Ouseley (Dr. O. Gogarty) . . . Starkey in going out said, 'I am too full of indignation that the best piece that ever was in the Abbey should have been ruined by bad playing.' Most people thought it was a too long drawn out skit with clever ideas and sayings dotted here and there."

Not long afterwards came a mischievous report of Sir Horace Plunkett's death in America, filed, apparently, by a frustrated reporter. Gogarty duly noted the incident for later use in "Sackville Street". "Sir Horace was dissatisfied with his death, of which the press notices were quite unworthy. He had just died in New York, so that his loss would be all the greater to Ireland, which could not compensate itself by a public funeral. But, so inadequate were the obituaries that, without waiting for the Irish mail, he wrote on the fourth day to the newspapers pointing out the omissions and misunderstandings, and assuring 'those who worked with him' that the announcement of his death was premature, but that they and his country would have whatever years were left to him, devoted selflessly to their service."[5]

With the exception of *The Incurables*, which was never performed, and a surviving fragment of *Wave Lengths*, Gogarty forsook the stage as a mode of expression. Indeed, in a letter to Seumas O'Sullivan in the early 'twenties, he confirmed his renunciation of the theatre. "I want none of my stuff which was written to serve the Abbey of the moment resurrected."[6] Nonetheless, that fragment of *Wave Lengths*, in which the creator of the "voice machine" refuses to allow his invention to be used to make "a show of some poor silly mortal whose youth or whose tongue ran away with him," has its own significance. It has been held as evidence of Gogarty's rejection of his portrayal in *Ulysses*, an oblique acknowledgement of Joyce's success in perpetuating in print Gogarty's verbal excesses of years past. In James Carens' words that recreation of his youthful persona was destined to attach to him "almost with the force of a bardic curse – an identity that he came to loathe."[7]

When pressed on the whereabouts of *Wave Lengths*, Gogarty was to reply "unaccountably it is lost." Fortunately, sufficient survived to substantiate Professor Carens' contention. "Madam, our remedy is absolute. Absolute. Once the etherial voices are gathered and canned. I mean preserved, I mean absorbed. They never can be collected again just as the scent of the rose can never turn back into the flower. And as nothing grows or increases that is to say increments in the ether no method known to man can bring the words you uttered out of the air again. Once you have purchased your Wave Length."

CHAPTER THIRTY

In an atmosphere of increasing violence and disorder Oliver Gogarty pursued his various careers of surgeon, physician, polemicist, playwright, patriot and family man in his native Dublin and otherwise in Connemara. Over in Zurich his erstwhile friend and crony found himself revising now against a deadline episodes of the book that not even Nora thought likely ever to see the light of day. Ezra Pound, who had taken Joyce up as a cause, had switched allegiance from Harriet Monroe's *Poetry* to the more progressive and prose-oriented *Little Review*, run by Margaret Anderson and Jane Heap. On receiving the first chapter of *Ulysses* – "Telemachus" – in December 1917, Pound responded to Joyce. "Wall, Mr Joice, I recon you're a damn fine writer, that's what I recon'. An' I recon' this here work o' yourn is some concarn'd literature. You can take it from me, an' I'm a jedge."[1]

Three years Joyce's junior, Ezra Weston Loomis Pound was born into a Quaker family in Idaho. He left his native America in 1908, moving to London, his home for the following twelve years. He is held to have exercised a major influence on his fellow-exile T. S. Eliot, while being particularly drawn to the works of both Robert Browning and W. B. Yeats. All of which makes the above prose style the more difficult to reconcile or comprehend. Besides being a co-founder of the Imagist school of poets, Pound also championed Modernist writers, among them Percy Wyndham Lewis, the ill-fated Henri Gaudier-Brzeska, who sculpted an enormous bust of Pound, and, most notably, James Joyce. Pound subsequently moved to Paris and thence, in 1924, to Italy, where he found himself interned by the American army in 1948 for suspected Fascist sympathies. Deemed unfit to stand trial, he was incarcerated in Washington DC for ten years. Pound was released in 1958 and returned to Italy, dying there in 1972. Eliot considered that his collaborator suffered from being simultaneously "objectionably modern" and "objectionably antiquarian". A more dispassionate critic summarised Ezra Pound as being "widely accepted both as a great master of traditional verse forms and as the man who regenerated the poetic idiom of his day."[2]

Where Joyce and his *magnum opus* were concerned, Ezra Pound's decision to change publishers proved inspired. Margaret Anderson went into raptures on receiving the third episode – "Proteus", with its introductory words, "Ineluctable modality of the visible . . ." The good woman was overwhelmed. "This is the most beautiful thing we'll ever have. We'll print it if it's the last effort of our lives." The first episode was published in the March issue of the *Little Review*. John Quinn, New York lawyer, intimate friend of Lady Gregory and patron of Irish art and artists in all disciplines, professed himself horrified at the language contained in the first episode. Pound sprang to the defence of his protégé. "I can't agree with you about Joyce's first chapter. I don't think the passages about his mother's death and the sea would come with such force if they weren't imbedded in squalor and disgust." However, Pound did admit to having deleted some twenty lines of the fourth episode "Calypso" on the grounds of excess. In this instance Joyce swallowed his professional pride, vowing to himself that *Ulysses*, when it should appear in book form, would be abridged, bowdlerised or censored by no man, or woman.

As he revised successive sections of his book for serialisation in the *Little Review*, Joyce showed them firstly to a new-found friend, regarded by those who knew both men as being as close a confidante of Joyce's as J. F. Byrne had been during Joyce's Dublin years. Frank Budgen, likewise born in 1882, had overcome a rudimentary education by reading widely while working as a seaman. He had subsequently gone to Paris to become a painter and supported himself by modelling for the Swiss sculptor August Suter. At the outbreak of war Suter persuaded Budgen to accompany him to his neutral homeland, where the latter secured a minor post in the British Consulate in Zurich. On their initial encounter Joyce had taken Budgen for a government spy. By his disarming manner, avid interest in literature, partiality to drink and aversion to anything remotely approaching hard work, Frank Budgen rapidly gained the lonely writer's confidence. No mean achievement this; and greater still to have sustained the trust and limited affection of which Joyce was capable. Frank Budgen later committed his memoirs of their association to print, in *James Joyce and the Making of Ulysses*, published in 1934.

"What do you think of Buck Mulligan in this episode?" said Joyce when I returned the typescript [of "Scylla and Charybdis" – Library scene].

"He is witty and entertaining as ever," I said.

"He should begin to pall on the reader as the day goes on," Joyce said.

"The comic man usually wearies," I said, "if he keeps it up too long. But I can't say that Buck Mulligan wearies me."

"And to the extent that Buck Mulligan's wit wears threadbare," Joyce continued, "Bloom's justness and reasonableness should grow in interest. As the day wears on Bloom should overshadow them all."

"But Bloom?" I said. "In this episode he hardly comes in at all."

"Bloom is like a battery that is being recharged," said Joyce. "He will act with all the more vigour when he does reappear."[3]

Budgen's book is primarily devoted to *Ulysses*, as he observed its creation in Zurich, while the rest of Europe and the Balkans were ravaged by war, and then, in his view at least, disillusioned and betrayed by the negotiated peace. There are, however, other occasional insights. In 1919, with the world war ended, the struggle for Irish freedom began to make international news. Budgen was curious as to Joyce's views. The latter, who had initially taken his new friend for a spy, was non-committal. Budgen persisted, stating his own opinion. "All this fighting with Ireland is absorbing too much English energy. History is leading us up the garden. We are being ruined by politics. Let us give economics a chance. The Irish want political autonomy. Why not give them what they want, give them at any rate what will satisfy them? Then, perhaps, when history is satisfied, the two islands will be able to realise their unity on an economic basis."

Joyce was unmoved. "Ireland is what she is and therefore I am what I am because of the relations that have existed between England and Ireland. Tell me why you think I ought to wish to change the conditions that gave Ireland and me a shape and a destiny?"

When they did return to the subject, Joyce turned the discussion to the only aspect he felt mattered – *Ulysses*. "I wonder what my own countrymen will think of my work?"

Budgen was candid. "I think they won't like it. The ardent party man is apt to believe that he who is not with him is against him. He understands opposition, but doesn't like criticism. Your countrymen are men of violent beliefs, and your book is the book of a sceptic."

"I know it is. It is the work of a sceptic, but I don't want it to appear the work of a cynic. I don't want to hurt or offend those of my countrymen who are devoting their lives to a cause they feel to be necessary and just."

Frank Budgen wrote his book soon after de Valera had plunged Ireland into what became known as the Economic War, when the newly elected Fianna Fail party decided to withhold land annuities due to Britain under the terms of the treaty of 1921. He can only have winced at his own simplistic solution to the "Irish question" as he had put it to Joyce some fourteen years previously. He may well have wondered, too, at Joyce's casuistry in their subsequent conversation, for *Ulysses* had but little or nothing to do with the "Irish question", as understood by Englishmen.

CHAPTER THIRTY-ONE

James Joyce might have been content with the status quo in the country he had left, but those who remained had other ideas. In the aftermath of the Armistice Gogarty wrote to Lady Leslie: 'The country is on the brink of rebellion.' The general election of December 1918 confirmed his view, though in a 'slightly constitutional' way. Sinn Fein, now encompassing much more militant factions, typified by such as de Valera, Michael Collins and Harry Boland, obliterated the old-fashioned, essentially loyalist Irish Party, taking 73 of the 105 Irish seats in Westminster. The Irish Parliamentary Party retained only six, a loss of 74, with the remainder going to the Unionists. If that were not enough, Sinn Fein promptly announced that its duly elected representatives of the Irish people would sit as a legislative and administrative body, not in Westminster, but in Dublin. At Dáil Éireann's initial assembly the hawks carried the day, emerging as the Irish Republican Army, reaffirming that republican aspiration of Easter Monday 1916, and using that mandate to engage in a very different form of insurrection. Under Michael Collins the IRA began to wage guerrilla warfare against the forces of the Crown, which included the Royal Irish Constabulary.

The British responded by deploying ex-servicemen – the Auxiliaries – and the Black and Tans, so-called after a celebrated pack of foxhounds because of their khaki jackets and black trousers. As it could not be seen to be a straight fight between the British military and an Irish insurgent army, this was portrayed in Westminster and the British media as a "police" campaign against armed gangsters. However, the British had no monopoly on propaganda, as the worldwide coverage of Terence McSwiney's 74-day hunger strike clearly demonstrated. The Lord Mayor of Cork had entered the fifth week of his political protest in Brixton prison. Mary McSwiney, his sister and an equally committed republican, was determined that the family should have a permanent memorial to her brother, whose death was feared imminent. She appealed to Gogarty.

Albert G. Power RHA had learned his sculpture under John Hughes and Oliver Sheppard, and his painting under William Orpen at the Dublin Metropolitan School of Art. Power had refused all Orpen's entreaties to move to England, in search of greater fame and fortune. Rather had he availed of his friendship with Gogarty, whom he had met through Orpen, to sculpt portrait busts of both Lord Dunsany and W. B. Yeats. Now, at Gogarty's request, Albert Power agreed to form part of a family group to visit the dying McSwiney in Brixton and make a likeness. The visitors were thoroughly searched before being allowed to enter. However, Power managed to secrete a small ball of wax between his fingers, while the officer searching him took the tiny wooden tools in his pocket to be matchsticks. Conscious of the eyes of the warder upon him from behind, Power knelt down beside the dying man, feigning a one-sided conversation, at the same time deftly shaping a wax impression of his emaciated features. McSwiney's ordeal came to its inevitable, tragic end on 25 October 1920.

Those who accompanied Albert Power on this remarkable mission described Terence McSwiney as thoroughly emaciated, which, after five weeks, was only to be expected. However, Power chose instead to portray an idealised version, along the lines of traditional depictions of Christ himself and the early Christian martyrs. In doing so Albert Power elevated Terence McSwiney to quasi-religious martyr, a victim of British injustice. Following McSwiney's death the story of Power's infiltration of Brixton became one of the major news stories in Ireland, accompanied by photographs of the plaster image. Fearing retribution by the British, Albert Power had several copies made and the marble effigy was hidden in Dublin until it was felt safe to present in to the McSwiney family in Cork. Albert Power was destined to receive further commissions through Gogarty, in particular Gogarty's friends and heroes, Arthur Griffith and Michael Collins.

Gogarty's nationalism had been inflamed not just by the events since the abortive rising of 1916, with its resultant blood-letting, but by the wanton brutality and gratuitous violence of the hoodlum forces despatched to Ireland by the British government. He was not alone, as evidenced by these words from none other than General Sir Hubert Gough.

"Law and order have given place to a bloody and brutal anarchy in which the armed agents of the Crown violate every law in aimless and vindictive and insolent savagery. England has departed further from her own standards, and further from the standards even of any nation in the world, not excepting the Turk and the Zulu, than has ever been known in history before."

Gough's opinion carried particular weight in the context of his own experience, for he it was who had reluctantly headed what became known as the "Curragh mutiny" in March 1914. He and officers under his command had been issued an ultimatum – prepare to take up arms against Ulster Unionists, or resign your commissions. Almost to a man Gough and his officers had opted for resignation. Gough's subsequent removal from command of the 5th Army in 1918 was attributed by many to "certain elements of the government" avenging themselves for Gough's perceived disloyalty four years earlier. "Thruster" Gough, though regarded by the Commander-in-Chief, Field Marshal Haig, as the most dashing of his commanders, was replaced by General Birdwood, and thereafter remained without a command until his retirement in 1922. His statue – the Gough monument – in the Phoenix Park was so frequently the object of incendiary practice that it was eventually removed.

While the more enlightened among British politicians began to advocate a united Ireland as a more stable and sustainable entity, the Ulster Unionists were having none of that. Eventually the nine counties comprising the province of Ulster were narrowed down to six, regarded as predominantly Protestant. This was hard luck on the Catholic majority who happened to live in Fermanagh, Tyrone and Derry City. They found themselves swept into the religion-based apartheid that is Northern Ireland, while the denizens of Donegal, Cavan and Monaghan were consigned to take their chance in the emergent Free State.

That political and economic entity came closer to reality in the aftermath of elections In May 1921, following an agreed cease-fire in January. Sinn Fein swept the board once again, with 124 seats, while the Unionists devised tactics that would become their trademark to ensure a total of 40 seats. The following month King George V's speech at the opening of Parliament contained conciliatory elements penned for him by the South African leader, Jan Smuts, balanced by more belligerent contributions from Arthur Balfour. The wily Lloyd George had crafted the king's address as an olive branch to the Irish nationalists . . . A truce was declared, effective from 11 July 1921.

Earlier that month Arthur Griffith enlisted Gogarty's aid in his attempt to waylay General Smuts, who was crossing to Ireland on the night mail for a meeting with British officials in Dublin Castle. With Gogarty at the wheel of his Rolls-Royce, the party assembled outside the church in Lower Merrion Street in the early hours of the morning. The interception committee comprised Griffith, Gogarty, Robert Barton and Larry O'Neill, Lord Mayor of Dublin. They arrived on the pier as the mail boat was docking. Griffith's intended discretion was blown away when Larry O'Neill bounded up the gangway. "Tell General Smuts the Lord Mayor of Dublin wishes to greet him."

The passenger list appeared to confirm the steward's denial that any such person was on board. Eventually, when all passengers had disembarked, an apologetic Larry O'Neill asked Arthur Griffith where he would care to go next. "Number Five Merrion Square." Gogarty recognised the address of Dr Robert Farnan, a leading gynaecologist and professor of midwifery in University College. Having dropped his passengers, Gogarty went off to garage the Rolls, lest attention be drawn to betray his passengers' whereabouts to intelligence agents. On his return he found de Valera having breakfast with Dr Farnan. When the telephone rang it was Dublin Castle looking for de Valera . . .

"Is your car at the door?" came the obvious query.

"I'm not quite such a fool," was Gogarty's injured retort.

The call from the Castle was to arrange a meeting at the Mansion House between General Smuts and the Irish leaders. It transpired that the South African had concealed his presence on the mail boat in order to confer with the British before meeting the Irish cabinet. If that were not bad enough, Smuts' warning to the Irish leaders was succinct, and prophetic. "I tried a Republic and it was a failure."

During that same period in which open hostilities were suspended, but advantage was taken where it arose, Gogarty and his Rolls Royce were once again brought into play. The occasion was a jailbreak from Mountjoy, involving Linda Kearns and a group of prisoners, whom Gogarty drove to safety at rare speed from Cross Guns Bridge. Nevertheless, it was in providing the social platform between his friend Arthur Griffith and Unionists such as Lord Dunsany and his cousin Sir Horace Plunkett at 15 Ely Place that Gogarty, in the opinion of General Richard Mulcahy, proved most valuable. That Ely Place should have been a "safe house" for Michael Collins when he was the most wanted man in the British Empire, was quite another matter. As Brenda, Gogarty's daughter later recalled, her parents occasionally voiced their concern that she might talk at school about the strange man she had seen in her house. Discretion learned in childhood was to stand Brenda in good stead in another time of world conflict. She needed no reminding that "Careless talk costs lives", for well she knew it.

Brenda could hardly have known that it was her father's perceived threat to her safety that had induced him to throw in his lot with Michael Collins and the republican cause. That story – like so much of Gogarty's personal life – remained untold for many years. It was not until 1952, when asked for his contribution to the newly-founded Irish Military Archive, that Gogarty divulged the circumstances that decided his active commitment to the nationalist cause. Writing from New York to Michael McDunphy, Director of the Bureau of Military History in Dublin, Gogarty outlined his conversion from pacifism, as advocated by Arthur Griffith, to activist supporter of the militant Michael Collins.

"Dear Mr McDunphy, When the Black and Tans behaved in such an excited and unsoldierly way by endangering my daughter's life when she was playing in St. Stephen's Green, I resolved to give all the help in my power to the Resistance movement headed by Michael Collins. His confident, Batt O'Connor was a patient of mine. To him I gave whatever gold I could come by for his reserve which was in a metal box cemented into a wall at Donnybrook where Batt O'Connor was building at the time. I also gave him a latch key of my house, 15, Ely Place and prepared that apparently impassable cul de sac so that Collins, if hard pressed, could use my garden and appear in St. Stephen's Green. There was a passage between the Board of Works and the Church Representative Body house that, through a wicket, gave on to the Green. In order to facilitate the scaling of the wall I had some cases of petrol placed against it under a large ash tree in the garden. These preparations were passed on by Batt O'Connor to Michael Collins and his thanks conveyed.

Collins was an infrequent caller at my house.

Emmet Dalton handed me back the latch key which he took from the blood-stained tunic of General Collins, who was murdered by the instigator of the Civil War.

You are at liberty to make whatever use of this you may find good.

Believe me to remain, with every good wish for you and the work,

Yours sincerely,

Oliver St. John Gogarty"[1]

That Gogarty, a close friend of Arthur Griffith, should have been influential in securing the release from captivity of his equally close friend Lord Dunsany, a prominent Unionist, through his influence with Dublin Castle, was a fair summary of the chaos and confusion that existed in Ireland at the time. And while Trinity College, Gogarty's alma mater, remained of course aloof and withdrawn from the political and martial turmoil that surrounded it, the role of one of its more controversial alumni did not go unnoticed. Indeed, the then provost, Dr Bernard, was overheard informing the Viceroy to the effect: "Gogarty is the most dangerous intellect unapprehended in Ireland."[2]

CHAPTER THIRTY-TWO

If Gogarty heard anything of Joyce and his doings during this period of political and military upheaval in Ireland, it will only have been to the effect that Joyce intended to pillory Gogarty and others in *Ulysses*, his long-awaited "masterpiece". Until such time as that book reached its conclusion, no one who featured in it could rest easy. But then neither could the author, as correspondence to Harriet Weaver made plain. Having disclosed his fear that successive episodes would "alienate gradually the sympathy of the person who is helping me", he went on to reveal that he had only to draw another character into the story for some awful misfortune to befall the real life person on whom the denizen of *Ulysses* was modelled. Worse, Joyce's absolute refusal to yield to the demands of Mrs Edith Rockefeller McCormick, his other principal benefactress, that he subject himself – even at her expense – to analysis by Carl Jung, saw his allowance from that quarter cease abruptly, never to be renewed. "As the Bank told you, I am not able to help you any longer financially, but now that the difficult years of the war are past, you will find publishers and will come forward yourself, I know. Wishing you a good journey, Sincerely, Edith McCormick." Thus did a considerably chastened and impoverished James Joyce return to Trieste after four years in Zurich.

Awaiting the return of James Joyce and his family to a crowded post-war Trieste were his brother Stannie, his sister Eileen and her husband Frantisek with their two small children. Frantisek had regained employment, as had Stannie, recently released from internment. For various reasons none of them looked forward to reunion with James and his family, not least because what was a comfortable apartment would necessarily become over-crowded. And Stannie had his own, personal reasons for wishing to make his own way in life, away and apart from his older brother's dissolute shadow. Besides, even if Stannie were content to resume his former role as his brother's keeper, James made it plain that his relative affluence made him both independent and resentful of Stannie's role as "my brother's keeper." Time had moved on.

Attempts to resurrect the interrupted *Ulysses* seemed somehow doomed in the absence of Frank Budgen as confidante and advisor. Casting around for both material and inspiration, Joyce resorted to writing back to his aunt Josephine Murray in Dublin for novelettes and a penny hymnbook, as well as verification of certain topographical aspects of Dublin. Ironically, Joyce's letters to Frank Budgen, in which he implores him to come to see him in Trieste, offering to contribute to the cost, are so similar in style and whimsy to summonses from Gogarty to Joyce almost twenty years earlier that they could have been written by Gogarty. When Budgen revealed that London or Cornwall would do more for his prospects as a painter than Trieste, Joyce immediately contemplated returning via London to see his father again and then summering in Ireland, but for the Black and Tan atrocities. Joyce was mortally afraid of gunfire. Instead Joyce, Nora and their children Giorgio and Lucia travelled to Paris for a week. And remained for twenty years. On leaving Trieste behind him, Joyce similarly discarded brother Stannie, though they did correspond intermittently.

Returning to Paris almost twenty years after his initial foray there to study medicine, Joyce found himself welcomed as now as something of a literary lion, immediately put on a pedestal by the booksellers Sylvia Beach and Adrienne Monnier. The financial stability provided by the selfless Harriet Weaver allowed Joyce to re-write the "Circe" episode of *Ulysses* numerous times, although the prospects of getting it published in book form seemed as remote as ever. Through Ezra Pound Joyce had struck up a form of friendship with T. S. Eliot and Wyndham Lewis, but even their contacts were of no avail and Joyce remarked to Pound that no country outside Africa would print his book. Many's the true word spoken in jest. Who could ignore the fact that the United States Post Office had already seized and burned no fewer than four issues of the *Little Review*, specifically because they contained episodes of *Ulysses*. In the obscenity trial, staged in New York in February 1921, John Quinn, who had been buying the episodes piecemeal from Joyce, defended Margaret Anderson and Jane Heap, publishers of the *Little Review*. His initial line of defence argued that episodes read out of context could be construed as offensive – in the sense of vulgarity as distinct from obscenity – whereas they were not so if read in the context of the book as a whole. The publishers were fined $50 each for publishing obscenity and saved only from prison sentences by Quinn conceding that the "Nausicaa" episode was the worst in the book, publication of which was henceforth banned. The case and its outcome inevitably attracted media attention, welcomed by some in terms of "all publicity is good publicity", always and ever debatable. Only later did the real consequences emerge. By virtue of the Court's ruling *Ulysses* could not be copyrighted in the USA by integral publication. This in turn was to give rise to an unauthorised and mutilated version being circulated.

When all was doom, gloom and despondency, Sylvia Beach sprang into the breach, offering to publish a limited, subscription edition in French under the Shakespeare imprint. Joyce could hardly conceal his surprise and delight, and promptly agreed. Quite carried away now, Sylvia Beach offered Joyce a staggering royalty – 66% of the profits. Harriet Weaver undertook to furnish a list of all those who had enquired about obtaining *Ulysses* in England, in addition to sending the author a further £200 as an advance on royalties of the English edition, which she proposed to print under the Egoist Press imprint as soon as the French edition of 1,000 copies, at three different prices, had sold out. The Egoist edition was published in October 1922, printed in Dijon and distributed from Paris by John Rodker, whose name appeared on the title page as publisher, for Egoist Press, London. The English edition ran to 2,000 copies.

However, the book remained unfinished, with awful misfortunes afflicting a whole series of typists secured by Sylvia Beach for the "Circe" episode. In one instance the typist's English diplomat husband was so appalled by what his wife was being asked to type that he threw the manuscript into the fire. Increasingly concerned, Harriet Weaver queried Joyce's drinking habits . . . Identifying her informants as Wyndham Lewis and Robert McAlmon, Joyce penned a lengthy and spirited rebuttal. While conceding that "excess" was a relative term and acknowledging Lewis's sincere offers of help, Joyce momentarily lifted a veil. "There is a curious kind of honour-code among men which obliges them to assist one another and not hinder the free action of one another and remain together for mutual protection with the result that very often they wake up the next morning sitting in the same ditch."

Towards the end of this amusing, cleverly evasive screed of refutation, Joyce alluded to another undercurrent within a sometime friendship. "I forgot to tell you another thing. I don't even know Greek though I am spoken of as erudite . . . I spoke or used to speak modern Greek not too badly (I speak four or five languages fluently enough) and have spent a great deal of time with Greeks of all kinds from noblemen downwards to onionsellers, chiefly the latter. I am superstitious about them. They bring me luck."

While still making alterations to the last two episodes – "Ithaca" and "Penelope" – Joyce simultaneously abjured Sylvia Beach and Maurice Darantiere, master "intellectual" printer, to have copies available by 2 February 1922 – Joyce's fortieth birthday. Duly two copies arrived on the early morning train from Dijon, collected from the conductor by an excited Sylvia Beach in person. Appropriately they were bound in the Greek national colours, white on a blue background; a white island rising from the blue sea. Ulysses had been sixteen years in gestation and had taken long, wearisome years to write and re-write and juggle and correct and expand and amend, even to the issue of how the book should end. The final "Yes" was incorporated at the insistence of an inspired French translator, Jacques Benoist-Mechin.

CHAPTER THIRTY-THREE

As James Joyce struggled to finish *Ulysses*, his compatriots who formed the Irish delegation to London were engaged in an infinitely more deadly struggle – to turn the armed truce that had existed since July 1921 into a more permanent treaty that would see the end of British occupation of three-quarters of the island of Ireland after seven hundred years. As president of Sinn Fein, de Valera had elected to remain at home, contending that his presidential status meant that only the King of England could negotiate with him on level terms. Ominously, two remarks of de Valera's as he selected the Irish delegation revealed his underlying motives. He observed firstly the need to "get out of the strait jacket of the Republic" and secondly that "we must have scapegoats." The delegation comprised Arthur Griffith, Michael Collins, Eamon Duggan, Charles Gavan Duffy, and Robert Barton, whose cousin, Erskine Childers, accompanied the delegation in a secretarial capacity.

After weeks of wrangling and tortuous discussion – and always within pre-conditions that rendered an Irish Republic simply out of the question – Lloyd George issued his ultimatum on 5 December 1921. The Irish could sign up to a free state with dominion status, or face immediate resumption of hostilities. There was no choice. At 2.20am on 6 December both sides appended their signatures, Lord Birkenhead, answerable as he was to the Northern Unionists, observed to Michael Collins, "I may have signed my political death warrant." He hadn't. As for Collins, a soldier and not a politician, there was no dissimulation. "I may have signed my actual death warrant."

As James Joyce made his final alterations to *Ulysses*, some by telephone and others by telegram, Dáil Éireann ratified the Treaty by 64 votes to 57 on 7 January 1922. Three days later Eamon de Valera led the anti-Treaty faction out of Dáil Éireann. In doing so he embarked, knowingly and deliberately, on the road to civil war; that most loathsome of internecine conflict, setting brother against brother. A sow can – and does – eat her farrow, just as a mare can sometimes kill her foal, and both calamities are attributed to quirks of nature. But de Valera's premeditated sabotaging of the fledgling Free State was diabolical in its reckless, self-serving perversity. Gogarty had little time for de Valera and his followers.

"I could never countenance this euphemism, Irregulars. They were mostly town riffraff misled, or country dupes and discontents whom de Valera aroused when he found that his methods had landed him in a minority."

Nonetheless, the emergence of a liberated Ireland with his old ally Arthur Griffith as its president, coinciding with his own regeneration of the Irish conscience through *Ulysses*, appealed to Joyce, in funds once again through a further subvention from Harriet Weaver. Her investment in James Joyce now amounted to £8,500, as he loftily informed brother Stannie. Nora seized the moment to suggest a family trip to Ireland so that the children and their grandparents might become better acquainted. Coincidentally, Desmond Fitzgerald, Irish Minister of Information, suggested that Joyce should return to sample Ireland under Irish administration. Joyce was evasive in replying, "not for the present." Nora and the children did make the journey via London and then across the Irish Sea, only to find themselves under fire from both sides when fleeing Galway by train. When the family was safely reunited back in Paris, and not until then, did Joyce declare that the violence to which they had been exposed was in fact an assassination attempt upon him. In August 1922 Joyce travelled to London, with Nora, and met Harriet Weaver for the first time.

By then copies of *Ulysses* had become more widely available, so much so that Joyce could ask his niece Kathleen, then nursing in London, what her mother, Josephine Murray, had made of her presentation copy of his book. "Well, Jim, Mother said it was not fit to read." Joyce responded stoutly to the effect that if *Ulysses* wasn't fit to read, then life wasn't fit to live. However, his favourite aunt's opinion confirmed Joyce's intention to steer safely clear of his native land while his compatriots struggled with his re-creation of their soul, and with each other. In writing to his aunt that autumn, Joyce closed his letter by saying that a second edition of *Ulysses*; 2,000 copies published on 12 October, had sold out within four days.

CHAPTER THIRTY-FOUR

On the eve of that fateful Dail debate on the Treaty, a group assembled in 15 Ely Place. It included J. M. N. Jeffries, Professor E. H. Alton and Father Dwyer. Almost inevitably as classicists, their attempts to predict the future saw them resort to the time-honoured *Sortes Virgilianae*. Instead of recourse to a medium – be it spirit world or gazing into a crystal ball – a copy of the *Aeneid* is opened at random with a pointer. The line on which the tip of the pointer rests contains the answer to whatever question may have already been posed.

Gogarty duly produced a copy of Virgil's epic, giving the pointer – a key in this case – to Fr Dwyer, in accordance with the condition that the instrument should only be inserted by a child, a chaste person, or a priest. The first and most pressing question was of course: "What will happen to Arthur Griffith?" Fr Dwyer inserted the pointer and handed the volume to Professor Alton, who translated the phrase indicated: "Spurned by the gifts".

The ambivalence of that answer – if indeed an answer it was – excited even greater curiosity as to the fate awaiting de Valera. In any case, there could be no turning back, at this juncture. The wording agreed upon was: "What will de Valera do?" Gogarty recalled the moment vividly in *As I Was Going Down Sackville Street*.

"But lest I be thought to have forced the translation let me quote from the account of a disinterested commentator and his rendering of the Latin. 'Rouse thee now and with joyful heart bid thy young men arm themselves and move to the fray and destroy the leaders of the foreign oppressors who have settled on our beautiful river, and burn their painted ships. The might of Heaven orders this to be done.'"

Continuing his account of that ominous experiment, Gogarty recalled de Valera's remark to a Southern Unionist during the treaty negotiations, which de Valera had steadfastly refused to attend, "If the fighting starts again, the Southern Unionists will not be treated as neutrals. And many unpleasant things will happen." Not surprisingly, in the light of Virgil's responses to the first two queries, there were no further questions and the gathering duly dispersed.

History would confirm the hideous accuracy of that recourse to Virgil. De Valera did indeed bid his young men arm themselves and move to the fray. He also went on record as saying that his vision of Ireland as a republic would not be realised other than through a welter of Irish blood.

"If they accepted the Treaty, and if the Volunteers of the future tried to complete the work the Volunteers of the last four years had been attempting, they would have to complete it, not over the bodies of foreign soldiers, but over the dead bodies of their own countrymen. They would have to wade through Irish blood, through the blood of the soldiers of the Irish government and through, perhaps, the blood of some of the members of the government in order get Irish freedom."

De Valera's disregard for democracy and the will of the people was made very clear in a public rally in Dundalk in April. "We made it impossible for a British Government to rule in Ireland – we can make it impossible for an Irish Government, working under a British Government, to rule in Ireland." The following day, in Drogheda, de Valera abandoned all pretence of belief in majority rule. "Republicans maintain that there are rights which may be maintained by force by an armed minority, even against a majority." On 14 April the anti-Treaty forces seized the Four Courts.

It was during this unstable period, when everything that had been achieved by the Treaty and ratified by the Dail teetered on the brink of collapse, and in its aftermath threatened return to British rule, that Gogarty's acquaintance with Michael Collins ripened into friendship. During the dark days when Collins was on the run with a price on his head, 15 Ely Place had been one of numerous "safe houses" where Collins was sure of his welcome. Noll Gogarty would later recall answering a knock at the door one dark night, at a time when requests for admission were not guaranteed a response. The caller identified himself in a soft Cork accent. "Never mind who it is. 'Tis good company you're in, anyway."

Gogarty and Collins shared a love of Walt Whitman, cake, sweet tea and irreverence. The cake and sweet tea they sought and found on their frequent forays to Beechpark, the Cosgrave family home out in Templeogue in the Dublin foothills. William T. Cosgrave, then Vice-President in the Free State Government headed by Arthur Griffith, had been 'out' on Easter Monday 1916 and duly found himself interned in a British jail for his involuntary role in the armed insurrection. Although well aware of just how high the stakes then were, Cosgrave could only give in to the mirth and gaiety of his callers. "I often thought that that pair of rascals took more delight in shocking me than in talking serious business when they came out to tea."

On a more serious note, "W.T." paid his long-vanished visitors this tribute.

"I believe now that Collins was the greatest Irishman that ever lived; greater than Parnell, Hugh O'Neill or Brian Boru. He was only on the threshold of his career. He died with so much of his greatness in him, we will never know what he could have achieved. He had courage you see; so had Gogarty."

On 16 June, following a pact with the dissident, republican wing of Sinn Fein, brokered by Collins to Griffith's dismay, general elections were held in the Free State. The electorate signified its support for the Treaty and thus the Free State Government. Reassured by this popular mandate, Arthur Griffith, the President, stated: "If we are not prepared to fight and preserve the rights of the ordinary people, we should be looked upon as the greatest set of poltroons that ever held the fate of Ireland in their hands." The republican dissidents in the Four Courts were given an ultimatum – surrender before 4.00am. Wednesday, 28 June. There was no response. At 4.07am. the Free State Army began shelling the Four Courts.

The republicans capitulated within forty-eight hours, by which time the Four Courts had been reduced to ruins, as was the Public Record Office. Collins' personal anguish was exacerbated by a telegram from Winston Churchill, which concluded, "If I refrain from congratulations it is only because I do not wish to embarrass you. The archives of the Four Courts may be scattered but the title deeds of Ireland are safe."

By the time August was out Arthur Griffith was dead from overwork, defying Gogarty's strictures that might have seen him spared. Summoned to find his patient, friend and leader already dead, Gogarty expressed his anguish, while pointing the blame, in his elegy,[1] published in *An Saorstat, The Irish Free State*, 19 August 1922.

Michael Collins carried Griffith's coffin, only to meet his end in an ambush in his native West Cork before the month was over. Gogarty waited through that night to receive and embalm Collins' corpse on its return by sea from Cork, aboard the SS *Classic*. And as he waited Gogarty composed an elegy elegy to his fallen idol, ally, friend and fellow-Irishman. Entitled Michael Coileain[2] – "Multitudinous is their gathering, a great host with whom it is not fortunate to contend the battle-trooped host of the O Coileain.", it appeared in its four-verse entirety on the cover of *An Saorstat, The Irish Free State*, 30 August 1922, the next issue in fact.

On this occasion Gogarty sent for Albert Power to make a death mask, while Sir John Lavery painted the corpse reposing beneath the tricolour, which he entitled simply "Love of Ireland".

William T. Cosgrave was appointed head of government as Griffith's successor and duly appointed Dr Oliver St John Gogarty to the inaugural Irish Free State senate, in which W. B. Yeats agreed to serve but "AE" declined. The latter's reticence was quite understandable, for the anti-Treaty forces had declared that public representatives supporting the Emergency powers measures would be shot on sight. Kevin O'Higgins took over Collins' mantle, exhibiting all the courage and conviction of his predecessor. It was said that had Griffith lived, then Gogarty would have become the first Governor-General, for Griffith would never have worn Tim Healy. The assassination of Sean Hales TD in December saw the government forced to choose between law and order or anarchy. In reprisal republican leaders Rory O'Connor, Liam Mellowes, Richard Barrett and Joseph McKelvey were executed without trial.

Gogarty escaped with his life when diving into the Liffey in January 1923.

He had been abducted at gunpoint by the "Irregulars" that he so despised, who had every intention of killing him in retaliation for the government's execution of republicans. Frustrated in that attempt, the republicans subsequently torched Renvyle House. "Nothing left but a charred oak beam quenched in the well beneath the house. And ten tall square towers, chimneys, stand bare on Europe's extreme verge."

The only way to capture
What may not be express'd:
Turn it into rapture,
Turn it into jest [3]

On this occasion Gogarty was beaten to the punch. While he sought to purchase a pair of swans to present to the 'Goddess of the River' in gratitude for his safe delivery from certain death, William Dawson composed the following ballad:

Come all ye bould Free Staters now and listen to my lay,
And pay a close attention please to what I've got to say,
For 'tis the tale of a winter's night in last December drear
When Oliver St John Gogarty swam down the Salmon Weir.
As Oliver St John Gogarty one night sat in his home
A-writin' of prescriptions or composin' of a poem
Up rolled a gorgeous Rolls-Royce car and out a lady jumped
And at Oliver St John Gogarty's hall-door she loudly thumped.
"O! Oliver St John Gogarty," said she, "Now please come quick,
For in a house some miles away a man lies mighty sick."
Yet Oliver St John Gogarty to her made no reply,
But with a dextrous facial twist he gently closed one eye.
"O!, Oliver St John Gogarty, come let yourself be led."
Cried a couple of masked ruffians puttin' guns up to his head
"I'm with you, boys," cried he, "but first, give me my big fur coat
And also let me have a scarf — my special care's the throat."
They shoved him in the Rolls-Royce car and swiftly sped away
What route they followed Oliver St John Gogarty can't say,
But they reached a house at Island Bridge and locked him in a room,

And said, "Oliver St John Gogarty, prepare to meet your doom."
Said he, "Give me some minutes first to settle my affairs,
And let me have some moments' grace to say my last night's prayers."
To this appeal his brutal guard was unable to say nay,
He was so amazed that Oliver St John Gogarty could pray.
Said Oliver St John Gogarty, "My coat I beg you hold."
The half-bewildered scoundrel then did as he was told.
Before he twigged what game was up, the coat was round his head
And Oliver St John Gogarty into the night had fled.
The rain came down like bullets, and the bullets fell like rain,
As Oliver St John Gogarty the river bank did gain,
He plunged into the ragin' tide and swum with courage bold,
Like brave Horatius long ago in the fabled days of old.
Then landin' he proceeded through the famous Phaynix Park,
The night was bitter cold and what was worse, extremely dark,
But Oliver St John Gogarty to this paid no regard,
Till he found himself a target for our gallant Civic Guard.
Cried Oliver St John Gogarty, "A Senator am I,
The rebels I've tricked, the Liffey I've swum, and sorra the word's a lie."
As they clad and fed that hero bold, said the sergeant with a wink,
"Faith, then, Oliver St John Gogarty, ye've too much bounce to sink."

EPILOGUE

"That bloody Joyce that I kept in my youth has written a book you can read on all the lavatory walls of Dublin." In so many words did Oliver St John Gogarty acknowledge his unwanted prominence as Roland Malachi Mulligan in *Ulysses*. Nor was Gogarty alone in his condemnation, echoing as he did the reactions of George Bernard Shaw, Shane Leslie and the majority of Anglo-Irish writers. While *Ulysses* was not actually banned in Ireland at that time, neither was it available on general sale. Indeed, when A. J. Leventhal's appreciative review was accepted for publication by the *Dublin Magazine*, the printers refused to handle it. Aunt Josephine's opinion of *Ulysses* – "It is not fit to read" – clearly carried the day.

While Gogarty could not and never did deny either his erstwhile friendship with Joyce, or his identity as "Buck" Mulligan, he could and did take steps to distance himself from his traducer. Brinsley Macnamara recounted one such instance when Gogarty declined an attractive American offer to write a book about Joyce. "The reason he gave me for this showed the difference between the two men better than any other explanation that I know of. 'I just couldn't do it,' he said. 'The man was too sad. Joyce was the very saddest man I ever knew.'"

On 4 May 1939 *Finnegans Wake* was published, to mixed critical acclaim. Gogarty reviewed it for the *Observer*. "When I think of the indomitable spirit that plodded on, writing *Ulysses* in poverty in Trieste, without a hope of ever seeing it published, I am amazed by the magnitude of this work, every word of which in its 628 pages, twisted, and deranged in order to bring up associated ideas in the mind . . . The immense erudition employed, and the various languages ransacked for pun and word-associations is almost incredible to anyone unaware of the superhuman knowledge the author had when a mere stripling. In some places the reading sounds like the chatter during the lunch interval in a Berlitz school. Every language living and dead in Europe gabbles on and on."

In his review, which apparently pleased Joyce, Gogarty described *Finnegans Wake* as "the most colossal leg-pull in literature since McPherson's Ossian."While repeating Yeats' observation that "this kind of prose made any other colourless", Gogarty preferred to define it as "the language of a man speaking, trying to speak, through an anaesthetic. It is an attempt to get at words before they clarify in the mind." Frank Budgen related how Joyce seized upon Gogarty's "indomitable", "erudition" and "magnitude", citing them as evidence of Gogarty's former athletic prowess, with emphasis on staying power. Others, albeit with the twenty-twenty vision of hindsight, were to identify *Finnegans Wake* as both Joyce's confession and final act of contrition. Gogarty elected, then and always, to laugh in the face of adversity.

Within two years James Joyce was dead. He died in Zurich on 13 January 1941. On his desk at the time were two books. One was *I Follow Saint Patrick*, by Oliver St John Gogarty. The other was a Greek dictionary, for translation purposes. As Gogarty had observed so often in times past, "Joyce knew no Greek."

ENDNOTES

INTRODUCTION
1 *New Light on James Joyce* – Professor James Carens, 1969.

CHAPTER ONE
2 SIR OLIVER ST JOHN, Viscount Grandison, was a distinguished soldier and moderate statesman who accompanied Lord Mountjoy to Ireland in 1601. He took part in the Irish campaigns and was appointed a commissioner for the Plantation of Ulster in 1608. In 1614 he wrote: "The province of Connaught has only two corporations, the ancient monuments of the English conquerors, and is inhabited

only by English families and surnames; the one in Galway, a walled town and port of the sea, lately made a county, and governed by a Mayor and 2 Sheriffs; the town is small, but has fair and stately buildings, the fronts of the houses (towards the streets) are all of hewed stone up to the top, garnished with fair battlements in a uniform course, as if the whole town had been built upon one model. The merchants are rich, and great adventurers at sea. Their commonality is composed of the descendants of the ancient founders of the town, and rarely admit any new English to have freedom or education among them, and never any of the Irish. They keep good hospitality and are kind to strangers; and in their manner of entertainment and in fashioning and apparelling themselves and their wives, they preserve most of the ancient manner and state, as much as any town that I ever saw. The town is built upon a rock, environed almost with the sea and the river, compassed with a strong wall and good defences, after the ancient manner, and such as with a reasonable garrison may defend itself against an enemy." *The History of Galway*, Sean Spellissy.

[3] *A History of the Church of Ireland 1691-2001*, Alan Acheson.

[4] Oliver Gogarty to Shane Leslie, 15 November 1919, Bucknell.

[5] Spellissy, p.97

[6] Borderlands – Old Rutland Square – Mary O'Doherty.

[7] Ibid,

[8] Ibid,

[9] *It Isn't This Time of Year at All!* Oliver St John Gogarty.

CHAPTER TWO

[1] Register of Births, Dublin North.

[2] Deposition of Elizabeth Gogarty, New Orleans, courtesy of Stanley J. Gauchet.

[3] *The Neighbourhood of Dublin*, Weston St John Joyce.

CHAPTER THREE

[1] Syncope = temporary loss of consciousness caused by a fall in blood pressure – *Oxford Dictionary.*

[2] *Tumbling in the Hay*, Oliver St John Gogarty, p.116.

[3] Information courtesy of Stanley J. Gauchet, New Orleans. His mother was Diane Gogarty, a direct descendant of Patrick Fleming Gogarty. Dr Henry Gogarty was buried in St Brigid's cemetery, Glasnevin. Margaret Gogarty, his widow, subsequently became the only other occupant of Plot BH 18-19.

[4] Bartley Oliver to Oliver Gogarty, 14 December 1925, TCD.

[5] Dr Joseph A. Oliver to Oliver Gogarty, 24 March 1926, TCD.

[6] *The History of Galway* – Sean Spellissy, p.137.

CHAPTER FOUR
1   *Tumbling in the Hay*, Oliver St John Gogarty, p.249.
2   Ibid., p.293.
3   Mayflo to Oliver St John Gogarty, c. 1944, TCD.
4   *It Isn't This Time of Year at All!*, Oliver St John Gogarty, p. 39. Stonyhurst records show that Oliver St John Gogarty entered the school on 17 September 1892 and left on 15 May 1896.
5   Oliver St John Gogarty to Mary Owings Miller, 1954, Bucknell.
6   *It Isn't This Time of Year at All!*, Oliver St John Gogarty, p.39.
7   Henry Gogarty (b.1882) entered Stonyhurst 22 January 1894, left August 1900. Stonyhurst records show a 'Louis' (Richard Aloysius?) at the school January 1899 – December 1902, Stonyhurst Association Archives; Archivist David Knight.
8   *Oliver St John Gogarty; The Times I've Seen*, Ulick O'Connor, p.5.
9   *Oliver St John Gogarty: The Man of Many Talents*, J. B. Lyons, p.26.
10 *It Isn't This Time of Year at All!*, Oliver St John Gogarty, p.41.
11 *Oliver St John Gogarty:the Man of Many Talents*, J. B. Lyons, p.27.
12 *James Joyce: the Years of Growth 1882-1915*, Peter Costello, p.102.
13 *James Joyce*, Richard Ellmann, p.35.

CHAPTER FIVE
1   *Ireland Revisited*, Charles Graves, p.46.
2   Balrothery – at that time a village beyond Templeogue, to the southwest of Dublin. "In front will now be seen some remains of the high ridge called Balrothery Hill, where formerly stood the old, dilapidated village of Balrothery, now entirely cleared away by the levelling of this end of the road to Tymon Castle. For many years prior to its removal it was an unsightly and conspicuous object along this road, scarcely one of the houses having been fit for habitation, besides which its exposed position must have rendered it a very uncomfortable place of residence, so that it is not surprising that its inhabitants gradually abandoned it as other accommodation became available in the neighbourhood." *The Neighbourhood of Dublin*, Weston St John Joyce, p.225.
3   *Tumbling in the Hay*, Oliver St John Gogarty, p.116.

CHAPTER SIX
1   *Dublin Revisited*, Charles Graves, p.46.

CHAPTER SEVEN
1   *John Stanislaus Joyce*, J. W. Jackson & Peter Costello, p.52-59.
2   *James Joyce:The Years of Growth*, Peter Costello, p. 178.

[3] "Vintage Gogarty", BBC interview with W. R. Rodgers, 1949.

[4] *James Joyce: The Years of Growth*, Peter Costello, p.193.

[5] Ibid., p.198.

[6] *Silent Years*, J. F. Byrne, p.84.

[7] W. R. Rodgers – D'Arcy O'Brien, p.88.

[8] "Vintage Gogarty", BBC Interview with W. R. Rodgers, 1949.

CHAPTER EIGHT

[1] *James Joyce: The Years of Growth*, Peter Costello, p.210.

[2] "Vintage Gogarty" – Interview with W.R. Rodgers, BBC, 1949.

CHAPTER NINE

[1] *The Dublin Diary of Stanislaus Joyce*, p.21-30 and footnotes.

CHAPTER THIRTEEN

[1] *Oliver St John Gogarty: The Collected Poems and Plays*, A. Norman Jeffares, p.387.

[2] *The Dublin Diary of Stanislaus Joyce*, p.69.

CHAPTER FOURTEEN

[1] William Bulfin – native of Birr, County Offaly. Emigrated to Argentina at seventeen, becoming gaucho, editor and newspaper proprietor in Buenos Aires. Returned to Ireland 1902, travelling the country by bicycle to collect material for his *Rambles in Eirinn*. Died Birr 1910. His daughter, Catriona, married Sean MacBride, founder of Clann na Poblachta.

[2] *James Joyce*, Richard Ellmann, p.174.

[3] *Leinster, Munster and Connaught*, Frank O'Connor, p.30.

CHAPTER FIFTEEN

[1] *Oliver St John Gogarty: The Collected Poems and Plays*, A. Norman Jeffares, p.461.

CHAPTER SIXTEEN

[1] *Oliver St John Gogarty: The Collected Poems and Plays*, p.413.

CHAPTER SEVENTEEN

[1] 'Ringsend' ref. *Oliver St John Gogarty: The Collected Poems and Plays*, p. 111.

[2] *Oliver St John Gogarty: The Man of Many Talents*, J.B. Lyons, p.57.

[3] Ibid.

[4] *Oliver St John Gogarty: The Times I've Seen*, Ulick O'Connor, p.94.

[5] Irish Military Archive, Witness Statement No.268.

[6] *It Isn't This Time of Year at All!*, Oliver St John Gogarty, p.97.

CHAPTER EIGHTEEN
1 *Dublin 1910-1940: Shaping the City & Suburbs*, Ruth McManus, p.401.
2 Seumas O'Sullivan to Oliver St John Gogarty, ND, Bucknell.

CHAPTER NINETEEN
1. Oliver St John Gogarty to Desmond Williams, 1 June 1956, ref. *The Renvyle Letters*, p.281.

CHAPTER TWENTY
1 *Oliver St John Gogarty: The Collected Poems and Plays*, A. Norman Jeffares, p.466.
2 Gogarty's father, Henry, died aged 49. His grandfather, James (d. 1851), had predeceased his own father, who died (1853) at 63. Thus Gogarty's concern about hereditary life expectancy, as expressed in a letter to an American cousin, Margaret Burke, 25 May 1924. "I have copied out a very interesting document which I got from New Orleans. It takes us back five generations to old James Gogarty who died at 95 years of age. This is a good inheritance." Gogarty was to live to 79, while his son, Noll, reached 92.
3 Information from J.B. Lyons.
4 *The Collected Poems and Plays*, A. Norman Jeffares, p.91.
5 Convent records, Convent of Mercy, Clifden, County Galway.
6 Henry Gogarty to O.P.G. ND, TCD Archives.
7 Anecdote from Stanley J. Gauchet.

CHAPTER TWENTY-ONE
1 *It Isn't This Time of Year at All!*, Oliver St John Gogarty, p.103.
2 *James Joyce*, Richard Ellmann, p.277-8
3 *James Joyce*, Richard Ellmann, p.277-8.
4 Ibid.
5 *James Joyce's Odyssey*, Frank Delaney, p.44.
6 *James Joyce*, Richard Ellmann, p.282n.

CHAPTER TWENTY-TWO
1 *Dublin's Meath Hospital*, Dr Peter Gatenby, p.87.
2 *Oliver St John Gogarty: The Man of Many Talents*, J. B. Lyons, p.74-5.

CHAPTER TWENTY-THREE
1 *Lord Dunsany: A Biography*, Mark Amory, p.67.
2 Ibid.
3 *While the Sirens Slept*, Lord Dunsany, p.63.
4 *Lord Dunsany: A Biography*, Mark Amory, p.75.

[5] *While The Sirens Slept*, Lord Dunsany, p.117.

[6] *Rolling Down the Lea*, Oliver St John Gogarty, p.163.

[7] *Oliver St John Gogarty: The Times I've Seen*, Ulick O'Connor, p.148.

[8] Ibid,, p.162.

[9] *Orpen: Mirror to an Age*, Bruce Arnold, p.259.

[10] *Oliver St John Gogarty: The Times I've Seen*, Ulick O'Connor, p.143.

CHAPTER TWENTY-FOUR
[1] Oliver St John Gogarty to Seumas O'Sullivan, 15 October 1913, NLI.

[2] *Erskine Childers*, Jim Ring, p.144.

[3] *Between the Flags*, S. J. Watson, p.143n.

CHAPTER TWENTY-FIVE
[1] *Oxford Encyclopedic Dictionary*.

[2] *Oliver St John Gogarty: The Collected Poems and Plays*, A. Norman Jeffares, p.451.

[3] *Oliver St John Gogarty: The Man of Many Talents*, J. B. Lyons, p.324n.

[4] *Oliver St John Gogarty: The Collected Poems and Plays*, A. Norman Jeffares, p.493.

[5] Henry Gogarty to Oliver St John Gogarty, 20 November 1916, TCD.

[6] *The Irish Horse*, Vol XVIII (1950), p.201.

CHAPTER TWENTY-SIX
[1] Martha Gogarty to Oliver St John Gogarty, N/D, TCD.

[2] *Beyond the Twelve Bens*, Kathleen Villiers-Tuthill, p.142.

[3] Remark to the author, c.1980.

[4] Martha Gogarty to Oliver St John Gogarty, TCD.

CHAPTER TWENTY-SEVEN
[1] *James Joyce*, Richard Ellmann, p.416.

[2] *The Jerome Connexion*, Seymour Leslie, p.143.

[3] *Leinster, Munster and Connaught*, Frank O'Connor, p.239.

[4] *John Stanislaus Joyce*, John Wyse Jackson and Peter Costello.

CHAPTER TWENTY-EIGHT
[1] *Oliver St John Gogarty; The Collected Poems and Plays*, A. Norman Jeffares, p.227.

[2] *Macmillan Dictionary of the First World War*, Pope and Wheal, p.104.

CHAPTER TWENTY-NINE
[1] *It Isn't This Time of Year At All!*, Oliver St John Gogarty, p.224.

[2] *Oliver St John Gogarty: The Man of Many Talents*, J. B. Lyons, p.115.

[3] Oliver St John Gogarty to Horace Reynolds, 9 February 1956, Harvard.

[4] *Oliver St John Gogarty: The Collected Poems and Plays*, A. Norman Jeffares, p.507.

[5] *Horace Plunkett,* Trevor West, p.186.
[6] Oliver St John Gogarty to Seumas O'Sullivan N/D [c.1923], Humanities Research Center.
[7] *Surpassing Wit*, James F. Carens, p.49.

CHAPTER THIRTY
[1] *James Joyce,* Richard Ellmann, p.421.
[2] *Oxford Companion to English Literature*, ed. Margaret Drabble.
[3] *James Joyce and the Making of Ulysses*, Frank Budgen, p.118.

CHAPTER THIRTY-ONE
[1] Irish Military Archive, Witness Statement No. 700.
[2] *As I Was Going Down Sackville Street*, Oliver St John Gogarty, p.273.

CHAPTER THIRTY-FOUR
[1] *Oliver St John Gogarty: The Collected Poems and Plays*, A. Norman Jeffares, p. 493.
[2] Ibid., p.494.
[3] 'Applied Poetry', see *Oliver St John Gogarty: The Collected Poems and Plays*, p.142.

BIBLIOGRAPHY

ACHESON, Alan – *A History of the Church of Ireland 1691-2001*, APCK, Dublin 2002

ALEXANDER, E. P. – *A Revolutionary Conservative,* Columbia, USA, 1938

AMORY, Mark – *Lord Dunsany:a Biography*, Collins, London, 1972

ARNOLD, Bruce – *Orpen:Mirror to an Age,* Jonathan Cape, London, 1981

BUDGEN, Frank – *James Joyce etc.,* Grayson & Grayson, London 1937

BYRNE, J. F. – *The Silent Years,* Farrar, Strauss & Young, New York, 1953

CARDOZO, Nancy – *Maud Gonne,* Victor Gollancz, London, 1979

CARENS, J. F. – *Surpassing Wit,* Columbia U. P., USA, 1979

COAKLEY & O'DOHERTY, Editors – *Borderlands*, RCSI, Dublin, 2002

COOTE, Stephen – *W.B. Yeats,* Hodder & Stoughton, London, 1997

COSTELLO, Peter – *James Joyce etc.,* Kyle Cathie, London, 1992

DELANEY, Frank – *James Joyce's Odyssey,* Granada, London, 1983

ELLMANN, Richard – *James Joyce,* OUP, 1983

ELLMANN, Richard – *Yeats and Joyce*, Dolmen, Dublin, 1967

FERRIS, Kathleen – *James Joyce etc.*, Kentucky U.P., 1995

FINDLATER, Alex – *Findlaters 1774-2001,* A & A Farmar, Dublin, 2001

FINGALL, Elizabeth – *Seventy Years Young,* Collins, London, 1937

FINNERAN, Richard J. – *Anglo-Irish Literature,* MLAA, New York, 1976

FORESTER, Margery – *Michael Collins,* Sidgwick & Jackson, London, 1971

GATENBY, Peter – *Dublin's Meath Hospital,* Town House, Dublin, 1996

GIBBON, Monk – *The Masterpiece and the Man,* Rupert Hart-Davis, London, 1959

GIFFORD, Don –*Ulysses Annotated*, UCLA Press, Berkeley, USA, 1988

GLENAVY, Beatrice – *Today We Will Only Gossip,* Constable, London, 1964

GOGARTY, O. St J. – *As I Was Going Down . . .*, Rich & Cowan, London, 1937

GOGARTY, O. St J. – *Tumbling in the Hay,* Constable, London, 1939

GOGARTY, O. St J. – *It Isn't This Time of Year at All!*, Doubleday, USA, 1954

GOGARTY, O. St J. – *Rolling Down the Lea,* Constable, London, 1950

GRAVES, Charles – *Ireland Revisited,* Hutchinson, London, ND (1948?)

GWYNN, Stephen – *Dublin Old & New,* Browne & Nolan, Dublin, 1938

HOLLOWAY, Joseph – *Impressions of a Dublin Playgoer,* Univ. Sth. Illinois, 1966

HOLROYD, Michael – *Augustus John,* Vol II, Heinemann, London, 1975

HONE, Joseph – *W.B. Yeats,* Macmillan & Co., London, 1942

JACKSON & COSTELLO – *John Stanislaus Joyce,* St Martin's, USA, 1998

JEFFARES, A. N. – *O. St J.G. Collected Poems and Plays*, Colin Smythe, Gerrards Cross, 2001

JEFFARES, A. N. – *W.B. Yeats,* Gill & Macmillan, Dublin, 1996

JENKINS, Brian – *Sir William Gregory,* Colin Smythe, Gerrards Cross, 1986

JOHN, Augustus – *Chiaroscuro*, Jonathan Cape, London, 1954

JOHN, Augustus – *Finishing Touches,* Jonathan Cape, London, 1964

JOHNSTON, Denis – *Orders and Desecrations,* Lilliput, Dublin, 1992

JOYCE, Stanislaus – *Dublin Diary*, Cornell, New York, 1962

JOYCE, W. St J. – *The Neighbourhood of Dublin,* Gill & Son, Dublin, 1921

KAIN, Richard M. – *Dublin*, University of Oklahoma Press, USA, 1962

KIBERD, Declan – *Ulysses,* Annotated Penguin, London, 2000

KOHFELDT, Mary Lou – *Lady Gregory*, Andre Deutsch, London, 1985

LESLIE, Seymour – *The Jerome Connexion,* John Murray, London, 1964

LEVIN, Harry – *James Joyce,* Faber & Faber, London, 1944

LIDDY, James –*Esau My Kingdom for a Drink*, Dolmen, Dublin, 1962

LYNCH, Brendan – *Triumph of the Red Devil,* Portobello, Dublin, 2003

LYONS, J. B. – *James Joyce & Medicine,* Dolmen, Dublin, 1973

LYONS, J. B. – *Oliver St John Gogarty,* Blackwater, Dublin, 1980

LYONS, J. B. – *The Quality of Mercer's,* Glendale, Dublin, 1991

LYONS, J. B. – *Thrust Syphilis down to Hell,* Glendale, Dublin, 1988

LYONS, J. B. – *What Did I Die Of?,* Lilliput, Dublin, 1991

McCOOLE, Sinead – *Hazel: Lady Lavery 1880-1935,* Lilliput, Dublin, 1996

McMANUS, Ruth – *Dublin 1910-1940,* Four Courts Press, Dublin, 2002

NEGROTTI, Rosanna – *Joyce's Dublin,* Caxton, London, 2000

O'BRIEN, D'Arcy – *W.R. Rodgers (1909-1969),* Bucknell, Lewisburg, 1970

O LAOI, Padraic – *Nora Barnacle Joyce,* Kennys, Galway, 1982

O'BYRNE, Robert – *Hugh Lane 1875-1915*, Lilliput, Dublin, 2000

O'CONNOR, Frank – *Leinster, Munster & Connaught,* Robert Hale, London, ND

O'CONNOR, Ulick – *A Terrible Beauty is Born,* Hamish Hamilton, London, 1975

O'CONNOR, Ulick – *Celtic Dawn*, Hamish Hamilton, London, 1984

O'CONNOR, Ulick – *Oliver St John Gogarty*, Obolensky, USA, 1963

O'DOHERTY, Mary – *Borderlands (Old Rutland Square)*, RCSI, Dublin, 2002

PEARSON, Peter – *The Heart of Dublin,* O'Brien Press, Dublin, 2000

RING, Jim – *Erskine Childers*, John Murray, London, 1996

RUSSELL, George – *The Living Torch,* Macmillan & Co., London, 1937

SHERIDAN, John D. – *James Clarence Mangan,* Talbot Press, Dublin, 1937

SPELLISSY, Sean – *History of Galway,* Celtic Bookshop, Limerick, 1999

STANFORD & McDOWELL – *Mahaffy,* Routledge & Kegan Paul, London, 1971

WALLACE, Martin – *100 Irish Lives*, David & Charles, London, 1983

WEST, Rebecca – *1900,* Crescent Books, New York, 1996

WEST, Trevor – *Horace Plunkett*

WEYGANDT, Cornelius – *Irish Plays*, Houghton Mifflin, USA, 1913

WHELPTON, Eric – *The Book of Dublin,* Rockliff, London, 1948

WHITE, Terence de Vere – *A Fretful Midge*, Routledge & Kegan Paul, London, 1957

WILSON, T. G. – *Victorian Doctor,* Methuen & Co., London, 1942

INDEX